MW01611131

LIFE, YOGA
AND CANCER

LESSONS FROM THE
BATTLEFIELD

DAVID DANON

LIFE, YOGA AND CANCER

LESSONS FROM THE BATTLEFIELD

DAVID DANON

Copyright © 2017

All rights reserved. No part of this publication may be reproduced or distributed in any form or by any means, electronic or mechanical, or stored in a database or retrieval system without prior written permission from the publisher.

First edition 2018

lifeyogaandcancer.com

Front cover art by David Danon

Rear cover portrait by the amazing Natalia Fabia
nataliafabia.com

ISBN: 978-1732144408

Published by;
Authentic Underground Press
1835 Newport Blvd., Ste. A109-154
Costa Mesa, Ca. 92627

For my Mother who gave me yoga, and my Guru who gave me the path.

Table of contents

Foreword

On Thanksgiving Day 2015 I launched my blog. It seems both appropriate and ironic to begin a discourse that involved cancer on a day of thanks. I called it Life, Yoga and Cancer: Lessons from the Battlefield.

I had never been one to put myself out there much on social media. I find addiction to "likes" and attention seeking self-indulgent and strange, and throwing out a cute picture of your child, pet, or a sentimental memory when all else fails, a little desperate. But things change, and purposes change. It took a lot of consideration and soul-searching for me to do it, but there I was.

I have had a somewhat unusual life, and along the way have learned a lot. I sailed around the world when I was nineteen to twenty-one years old. I've spent forty years doing yoga and meditation, and twenty years teaching it. I've enjoyed more art, music, sports, and travel than I can remember. Amazing and beautiful friends, family, students, and material comfort - I've had them all.

I thought I had all the knowledge I would ever need to ride this lifetime into the sunset, but on July 30th, 2012 I was told that I had cancer. A whole new phase of learning was just beginning.

I traveled that path mostly alone, and until I began the blog, only a handful of people knew. I guess there was a certain "dramatic flair" to coming out the way I chose.

They say a blog should be focused on one clear niche. But if you do yoga, how can it be separate from your life? If you have a disease how can it be separate from your life and your yoga? It is all connected. All of it, and much more.

The chapters in this book have content related to life, yoga, cancer, and more. Many people start to write when they enter a crisis. They do it to keep their people informed, and possibly find therapy in it. That is so not for me. I am doing it so that maybe someone can find an answer that will help them.

I recently heard it said that "spiritual practice without service is just narcissism." I never had to, or wanted to teach yoga for a living. I just wanted to serve the best way I could. I was fortunate that I could be free of self-interest and stress that goes with promoting a business, and teach purely to serve the students.

I have always said that if every person could make a positive difference in just one or two other people's lives, what an amazing world this would be. I hope I have already been that person, but I'm not stopping now.

I have ended every yoga class I have ever given with these words: "Feel a moment of gratitude for all your blessings, most especially your health." You can probably imagine what I was thinking while saying that over the last few years. Yet I do feel gratitude for my health and all I have and have had. I wouldn't trade my life for anything.

Gratitude opens the channel between soul and spirit. It allows you to go where you need to go. Notice I said, "allows." Whether you choose to go there, or not, is up to you.

May your days be filled with Peace, Blessings and Good Health.

Introduction

"*I cannot teach anybody anything. I can only
make them think.*"-Socrates

With such an ambiguous title as Life, Yoga, and
Cancer, I thought it best to explain a little bit
about what this book is, why it came about,
and, what it is not.

Among the many catch phrases and buzzwords
these days, it is somewhat common to talk
about "mindfulness" and "setting intentions."
While I don't disagree with these sentiments, I
do think there is a time and place for different
strategies.

When going into any experience, be it a yoga
class or a new job, with an intention, one is
assigning a destination or an "attachment" to
the outcome of that experience. A "mindful"
approach may imply an intellectual precision to
the activity.

These are effective methods, but sacrifice
another aspect of the experience. That is
"improvisation" and embracing the "organic
evolution" of the experience.

To put it in musical terms, the former could be
compared to the concert musician playing his or

her part in the symphony with great precision and perfect technique, but no potential for change. The latter could be compared to a jazz or rock solo, which could go in any direction at any time.

The process of this book coming to be is the result of a single event - I was diagnosed with cancer. My reaction to that was to do what I have done over and over in life. I stepped into the flow of the experience, with eyes open, and improvised as I went along.

The more I dug in and researched, the more I learned about the disease and the system that treats it. Along with that, I experienced all the new emotional and psychological onslaughts that go along with a diagnosis like this. I dealt with it, basically alone, with the only tools I had: the commitment to research and learn everything I could, and my spiritual practice - my yoga.

As I mention in the book, I soon realized I was an anomaly. Choosing alternative medicine as a first choice is very rare. To do it from a yogic perspective is even more so. I thought the insights and information accrued might be of interest to others.

I started a blog:

- I wrote about the views of life that came from my new intimacy with my mortality.
- I wrote about Yoga, and how I felt about what it truly is and what it has become.
- And I wrote about cancer and what I had learned, firsthand.

I realized that the blog was just too cumbersome to navigate and access items of interest. The idea of the book was born. I have used material from the blog posts, as well as additional original content, and have separated information into sections.

This book is the result of an ongoing five-year mission, one I never imagined would be a part of my life.

What this book is not meant to do:

1. It is not a "how-to" regarding methods of treating cancer, although it mentions many.
2. It is not a "how-to" regarding methods of yoga or meditation, although it suggests possibilities.
3. It does not contain recipes or checklists, nor does it quote and reference a lot of scientific or medical studies or statistics.
4. It does not give medical advice.

What this book is meant to do:

- While this book deals with cancer, the approach and strategies are applicable to many other problems and challenges.
- It explains the value of a yogic/spiritual practice and the benefits and challenges related to that practice.
- It gives ideas, many based on my opinions and observations. You may or may not agree with them, but at least you will have had the opportunity to hear them before dismissing them.
- It suggests possibilities regarding cancer that may not be obvious. Possibilities of how and why it occurs and approaches to treating it and preventing it.

In yoga, it has been said that the "Demon of Ignorance" gets his power from the "quality of forgetfulness." This is such an amazing concept! It implies that we do not have to acquire "new and unknown" information to find relief and happiness in life. We only need to remember what we have forgotten.

Everything we need to achieve success and happiness is available to us, and within us, right now. But we must first recognize it and then apply the work involved.

And that, of course, is the catch - doing the work.

If we choose, for whatever reason, not to do the work, that is okay too. At least we have dumped the "victim mentality" and assumed some of the responsibility for our situation. And there is great value in that.

This is not a long book, and there is a reason for that. I have found, often in life, that truth can be expressed in the simplest of terms, or pontificated on for thousands and thousands of words. Many of the quotes peppered throughout this book are excellent examples of truth stated in the most concise and obvious way.

My intention has always been to try and express things, regardless of their complexity, in straightforward and understandable terms. That is often a challenge, but it is my goal - to "speak less, but say more."

To bring this back to a musical analogy, as you read through this material, open your mind to the concept of "improvisational" thinking. You don't have to agree with what I say or even like me. These thoughts are like sections from my "sheet music of life." You can view them through the eyes of preconceived "note for note thinking." Or, you can riff over them with your own new and original interpretations.

Play on!

Part One
Life

Chapter 1

Life

The Arena

Call it an arena. Call it a playground or playing field. It doesn't matter. It is the environment of your experiences.

Ever changing not only in terms of the day-to-day, but also in terms of the Era, Age, and foundation of the society prevalent at the moment.

The journeys, lessons, and challenges of those born in a "hunter/gatherer" society are far different from those born into an age of technology and atomic power.

Yet, the fundamental drive, motivations, and fears remain constant throughout all of life regardless of species, era, or society:

- Survival of the individual
- Perpetuation of the species
- Avoidance of pain
- Attraction to pleasure

Four basic impulses that can, easily, mutate into obsession, addiction, depression, and a host of other behaviors.

Most events of the day, or of life, are just "window dressing" that address, accommodate, or obstruct those objectives.

And when stripped of all its drama and "special effects" to its barest essence, it is really not that complicated.

Chapter 2

Why Does It Matter?

> *Knowledge is Power, but knowledge without action is useless.*

Some will ask, why does it matter? What difference does it make if I understand things about life? It will be what it is regardless of what I know or think about it, and I will deal with it.

Not quite true.

That is how it is when you are creating your environment in an unconscious default mode...because you are, in fact, continually creating the arena. If not consciously, then unconsciously.

It is being proven more and more, through quantum physics and neuroscience, that reality as we see it is inseparable from, and created by, the consciousness of the perceiver.

Creating your world is the subject of much New Age spirituality and psychology, and in fact, has roots going back to books from the early 20th century. It is just being repackaged for the new world of technology.

The obvious question is, "If people can create their realities, why aren't people living their lives with nothing bad, and only good?" That is a reasonable question, and the answer is because this particular arena exists in a universe that requires certain laws to sustain it.

The primary law, where we are right now, is duality. This arena cannot exist without opposites. It is the concept of Yin and Yang, two symbols separately representing opposites, but intertwined to create the whole.

So, yes, into every life some rain must fall. However, by an understanding of how things operate we can affect the degree of happiness and sorrow, joy and sadness, pleasure and pain.

Attachments, psychological programming during childhood by parents and friends, the culture and society we live in, and karma all affect the outcomes of our creation.

By understanding some mechanics of the "big picture" and our position on the field, we can, hopefully, give ourselves the best chance possible. A Chance for happiness and success.

"Anyone who stops learning is old, whether at twenty or eighty."- Henry Ford

Chapter 3

Having Fun

> "All the world's a stage, and all the men and women merely players..."- William Shakespeare

When my daughter was about three years old, she told me one day, "I had a dream about God." Well, I don't know about you, but when a three-year-old tells me she had a dream about God, I want to hear about it. So, I asked her what it was about. She said, "Well I was playing with my friends, and he came and was watching us." I asked her "Did he say anything?" She said, "He told us to have fun!"

I said, "Well if God told you to have fun, it's probably good advice!"

The conversation got me thinking about some aspects of fun and suffering in this journey of life. According to the teachings of Eastern spiritual practices, the true nature of the soul is love, joy, and bliss. This being the case, how did we get so far off track? How did we "stop having fun"?

Buddha tells us it is because of *attachment*. We acquire attachments, which leads us to desires, which leads us to identify our emotional state (both happy and sad) by how those desires are either satisfied or denied.From there it is a short trip to identifying ourselves with our desires, and who we are based entirely on our emotional state.

This is all helped along by "maya," the cosmic hypnosis. Through our containment in the different bodies (of which the emotions are a part), maya hides our true spiritual nature from us. We then identify ourselves as the body and our feelings, and many of us suffer greatly from this confused identity. However, it doesn't have to be this way.

As an actor takes on a different role and suffers or even dies in it, and yet enjoys the act of the performance, so are we actors in this cosmic play. Learning to control the power that emotions have over us is the mark of spiritual growth and evolution, leading to the path of enlightenment.

Anyone who is continually riding extreme emotional highs and lows, causing drama in themselves and those around them, but claims to be a "spiritual person" is deluded.

The actor can enjoy the performance of the tragedy because he knows himself as the performer. If he only perceives himself as the character he is playing, then his existence would be governed by the roles he plays.

And that is how most of us live. Our reality and feelings are determined by the temporary and ever-changing roles we play. To know our true nature as spirit is to know ourselves as the performer knows himself, and can help us to step away from the emotion of the role.

The more we identify and live in our spiritual nature the less affected we are by the emotional "noise" in and around us. It doesn't mean we can't play in the drama and have some fun. It means the drama does not control us.

This, however, does not mean that the role we play is unimportant or should be taken lightly. It is the job of the performer to please the director and always strive for an "Oscar-worthy" performance. It doesn't matter if it is raising a child or finding a cure for cancer. As the saying goes, "There are no small parts...."

I don't mean to imply that this is an easy thing to practice. It is not. It is the greatest challenge that we have in life. This challenge, the journey into enlightenment, is available to us 24/7, 365 days a year.

It sits, like a golden ticket, right behind our closed eyes, but we can't see it. We are unable to discriminate between the real and the unreal.

The value of a spiritual practice is not some pie in the sky reward to be had at some undetermined point. It is a process of realizing who we are as the performer and not the role we play. We do it through contact with the greater spirit within, and outside of, this creation. If we can accomplish this, then we can play like children, having fun.

There are many meditation techniques and yoga practices available to work towards this lofty goal. One size does not fit all, but at the core of it all, we must reshape our thinking and beliefs.

I believe that meditation and affirmation are essential in that practice. We must do the work until we experience what at first seems unreal, and know its truth. *The true reality that exists beyond and sustains this dream existence.*

Why is it so hard to maintain a focused practice? One reason is that we are so conditioned by high intensity, constant input of images and information, that the subtlety of the inner world doesn't hold our restless attention.

The only way out of this restlessness is self-discipline. The discipline to practice until it becomes a habit. The habit of taking the time to practice. Regularity and depth of practice yield results. Results to last a lifetime and into the next. The freedom to "have fun" regardless of the role being played.

Knowing there is a way to higher consciousness and being drawn to it is an intuitive experience. It cannot be bought, sold, scientifically proven or explained, because it exists beyond the confines of the intellect and the senses.

It is us, as the "knower," perceiving at the most subtle and refined level.

It is the first step on the yogic path.

Chapter 4

How Intelligent Are You?

> *"The true sign of intelligence is not knowledge, but imagination."*- Albert Einstein-

When I was young, I had a friend who was a genius. I remember, around the sixth grade, riding my bicycle up to his garage. He was in the process of putting his father's lawnmower engine back together after having taken it apart. I don't mean apart like a spark plug and a metal shroud. I mean down to the piston and small internal parts.

By seventh grade, he was "chopping" bicycle frames and doing custom paint jobs on them. By eighth grade, he was modifying engines for go-karts and mini bikes. After that, it was cars and motorcycles. Rebuilding and modifying engines, welding, custom paint.

His Christmas and birthday wishes were from the Sears Craftsman catalog... arc welder, metric socket set, compressor. I remember him proudly showing me his new torque wrench.

Where did this extraordinary talent lead? An in-demand race car mechanic? Custom car builder? Jay Leno's on-call mechanic? Well, no. He got into drugs and alcohol and drove his car off a cliff.

The reasons for this were probably several. However, having been there and seen it, I'm convinced of one thing that contributed to it. The relentless Ds and Fs in high school. I remember the anxiety and frustration on his face when report cards came.

I'm sure his lack of being gifted athletically in PE and being called a "motor head" by the jocks and cool guys didn't help either. God forbid that a gift like his should get any recognition in contemporary, conservative, high school.

Who can thrive in this world without positive reinforcement to their self-esteem? How many times can you be told "you suck" before you believe it, and then follow the path of self-medication to escape the "loser" persona that everyone says you are?

Our standard education system measures and rewards verbal-linguistic and logical-mathematical skills, with emphasis on memorization. This is what most schools consider and reward as intelligence.

Or, if you are an extraordinarily gifted athlete who can provide prestige to the school's sports program, then you will get some love there.

Unfortunately, if you are a person who has natural talents and abilities that lie outside the system's parameters, you are not acknowledged for them and are forced to try and excel at your weaknesses. This is the exact opposite of what should be happening.

The Nine Types of Intelligence.

In his 1983 book, Frames of Mind: The Theory of Multiple Intelligences, Howard Gardner proposed a model of multiple types of intelligence as opposed to the standard idea of intelligence dominated by a single general ability. These were not random, and he had specific criteria to determine if a particular ability qualified as a type of intelligence. He started with seven different types, and the list has since been expanded to nine. They are:

- Naturalist (nature smart) - In the past hunters and gatherers, now farmers botanists, environmental experts;
- Musical (ability to discern pitch, rhythm, tone, timing, etc.) - Composers, conductors, musicians;
- Logical-Math (we all know that one);

- Existential (an innate understanding/capacity to grasp questions pertaining to existence);
- Interpersonal (ability to understand and interact well with others) - Teachers, therapists, and even actors, politicians, and salespeople;
- Bodily-Kinesthetic (use a variety of physical skills and abilities) - Athletes, dancers, surgeons, craftspeople;
- Linguistic (the use of words and language to express complex meanings and ideas to others) - The most widely shared type of human intelligence exemplified by writers, speakers, poets;
- Interpersonal (To understand one's thoughts, feelings, and the human condition) - Psychologists, spiritual leaders, and philosophers;
- Spatial (picture smart - ability to think in three dimensions, spatial reasoning, graphic and art skills) - Painters, sculptors, sailors, pilots, architects.

This does not mean that we are born with only one of these types of intelligence. We all possess varying degrees of several or most of them. Most people, however, do excel naturally and with less effort in one or two of them. So what is the point of all this, and what does it have to do with my childhood friend?

If you were designing a civilization, would you want it populated entirely by people who were good at math and words? Would you only reward those people and disregard everyone else? Of course not. Who will fly your planes, design your buildings, fix your cars, and give you therapy when your skilled mathematical-thinking brain is flipping out?

Naturally, we don't treat our pilots, actors, musicians, and psychologists as second-class citizens. But the truth is many of them had to be born into families who, for whatever reason, recognized and nurtured their talents.

Either that or they had to have the wherewithal to figure it out at a young enough age and have the courage and commitment to say "Sorry, this is who I am, and I'm going for it."

The other obstacle that arises is that while there tends to be a prescribed "path" for those pursuing the status quo educational vocations as in business, media, accounting, science, etc., many other natural talents require a more creative or "entrepreneurial" approach to success. Not always an easy way to go.

So where does that leave you, me, and our children? For me, and maybe you, it is a little late. I know so much more now about the vocations that would have served my temperament better than the paths I stumbled through by necessity or default.

If you are living and thriving doing something that you were "born to do" - awesome! You are indeed fortunate. If not, perhaps you can find satisfaction using your true gifts in your hobbies or in a secondary source of income.

As for the children, try to find their innate unique types of intelligence. If it fits the public school paradigm, then great for you. You can "humble brag" to your friends.

If not, do what you can to provide the avenues for them to develop their talents. This doesn't mean that they forget school and grades. However, it does mean perhaps putting school and grades into a different context. Maybe consider school and study as a process of developing a work ethic and social skills that will serve them in life, as opposed to making it all about the grade.

Here is the bottom line and the takeaway of value. If someone's natural abilities and talents don't conform to the classic model of 'school intelligence", they are under pressure to become more proficient at something for which they are not naturally gifted. They try to "improve their weaknesses." As I stated at the beginning of this, that is the opposite of what someone should be doing to achieve their full potential.

Life is hard enough without wasting time traveling the path of most resistance.

The path to great success and happiness does not come from trying to gain skills in something that does not come naturally to us, nor has little meaning or relevance for us. It comes from developing and perfecting our natural abilities and delegating to others the things that are their skills and gifts.

This model of people's natural skill being identified, so that they perfect and excel at their natural talents, is not a novel concept. In many indigenous cultures throughout time, this has been the norm.

This does not mean that in this proposed world model everyone would be good or successful at what they do. Unfortunately, the hard work of developing, perfecting, practicing, and marketing these skills remains.

The hard work and dedication to perfecting one's natural gifts must still be done, and some can't do it. Maybe they are too lazy or too depressed. Perhaps too beaten down or too easily distracted. What are the options when this is the case? Maybe try to identify the problem, and delegate the help we need to someone whose natural skill is helping people with those types of issues.

Imagine that! A world full of people finding satisfaction with their vocation, with amazing competence, sharing their talents and gifts. Everyone respecting each other and grateful for each other's contribution to the collective.

And there is the word... "respect." Our culture loves to assign levels of value to different positions. It's all just that lame ego in action. Like somehow the big CEO in the big house is more relevant than the plumber. Forget that! Because when his toilet is overflowing in his big house, the CEO needs the plumber a whole lot more than the plumber needs him.

The more our society can find a connection in each other's value, and not look for petty reasons to discriminate based on skill set, income, possessions or titles, the better off we will be.

If you are making a living and finding happiness through your passion and gifts, you are so fortunate! Encourage, wish for, and respect that in all people, in all living things.

Chapter 5

Strange Days Have Found Us

> *"Toto, I've a feeling we're not in Kansas anymore." -Dorothy*

The times in which we are living have indeed brought strange mojo into our world. The age of technology has introduced contradictions and challenges unimagined 100 years ago.

In the recent past, new innovations were brought to us with the idea of "giving us more free time." Home-care items and appliances were going to be the answer to freeing up our time. We didn't know exactly what computers would do, but anything that could "compute" had to help make life easier, right? But what would we do with all that free time?

Well, in a yoga-based perfect world, the time would be spent pursuing activities which would satisfy our worldly obligations, promote our spiritual evolution, relieve human suffering, and promote the welfare of all living things. So, what went wrong, aside from the fact that we don't live in a "yoga-based perfect world?"

From the ego's standpoint, the activities mentioned above just don't sound like that much fun.

Sure, spiritual evolution sounds cool, but all that pesky meditation and whatnot, when I could be posting the awesomeness of my life on Facebook and Instagram. Oh, and getting likes! I could be texting three friends at the same time and getting so much done socially! I could be checking out all that "high-quality content" available on cable!

Oh, and of course, I need time for yoga, Pilates, and the gym. So much to do and so little time!

We are addicted to being busy.

It affects us exactly like a drug. The busyness takes us outside of ourselves. We can be distracted from the voice and emotions in our head that we live with when we are alone and quiet. The belief that being continually busy is the right thing to do is supported and sustained by our society. We are considered lazy or unproductive if we aren't busy being busy.

TV is a strange exception because in a way we are not busy, but we are distracted, and even better we are doing what we have been trained to do. We are "consuming." Because that is exactly what TV is, a consumable product, based on generating profit.

Why does this matter? *Because it takes us out of ourselves in the exact opposite direction from meditation and spiritual practice.*

Meditation and mindfulness are spiritual practices that take us out of ourselves in an *inward direction.* We detach from our senses and lose awareness of ourselves by connecting with something greater.

In busyness, we engage through our senses into the material world, and there lies the problem. The journey within is designed to lead us to something stable and consistent with qualities of love, peace, and bliss.

Outwardly the world throws us good and evil, happy and sad, up and down in a relentless nonstop barrage. While this seems enticing to the ego, it is destructive and unhealthy for us: for our body, mind, and soul. The more we partake in the fluctuations of the material world, and identify with it, the more we lose sight of our true nature, and the more we suffer. *We get ill: physically, mentally, and spiritually.*

I am not saying we should withdraw from all entertainment and diversions provided to us in this creation. I am saying to make time for loftier and more long-lasting rewards. Be productive and live a balanced life. Hold the intention to find a spiritual path, one that will lead you through this life in peace and growth. That is the measure of a quality life.

You don't want to be on your deathbed thinking, "Damn, why did I waste all that time staring at my phone, computer, and TV? I could have done so much."

Chapter 6

The Judge, the Victim, and the Meditation

> *"Judge not, that ye be not judged."*
> *- Matthew 7:1-3*

Last Sunday I went to a temple to meditate. It was a short meditation. By the time you get through the little pre-meditation talk, the prayer and the chant, there's only about a half-hour left of actual meditation time.

I occasionally go there because I believe in the power of fellowship, although the type of "fellows" involved does make a difference. I find temple meditations, nowadays, to be a little sketchy in terms of etiquette. You know, cell phones, coughing and sneezing, and evidently, even snoring.

About 15 minutes into the actual meditation one guy starts snoring. My first reactive response was, "Are you friggin kidding me? A half-hour meditation and you can't even stay awake for that? And now I gotta try to meditate listening to your inconsiderate ass snore?"

And there it was, as plain as day. The judge and the victim taking over in about five seconds.

In the book, The Four Agreements, Don Miguel Ruiz talks about the judge and the victim and how we operate through those personality traits. His take on this may vary some from mine but the bottom line, for me, is we are constantly judging every person, place, thing, and situation we encounter. Many of us are continually judging ourselves as well, although that is not the focus of this chapter.

While judging is not an innate spiritual trait, it is so pervasive that it is warned against in the Bible, "Judge not, that ye be not judged."

In addition to that, while we don't want to be considered weak, we love to be the victim. It exonerates us from any responsibility for our shortcomings in any situation in which we find ourselves. Even something as lame as "HIS snoring is screwing up MY meditation."

Fortunately, I saw it happen and adjusted my outlook. This has been a process I have had to consistently and consciously work on. To see a reaction happen, step back, and say, "This is a choice."

This is the work we need to do to free ourselves from the stress, anger, and anxiety this kind of reactive process creates within us. Because despite what the medical profession might have you believe, these emotional states will contribute to chronic disease, cancer included. So, what to do?

First, we need to commit to practicing constant objective vigilance in observing our mental state, and especially any reactive behavior. This is not easy. Our subconscious mind has a prime function to keep our conscious mind out of these habitual responses.

I am a big believer in affirmation having the power to intercede on behalf of the conscious mind and change subconscious behavior. Commit and regularly affirm, "I am constantly aware of my behavior" or "I observe and adjust my reactive behavior," or whatever resonates with you. This will help bring the conscious mind into the process.

Now this, of course, assumes that you feel a need to make these changes in yourself. If you are happy with the way you experience life and events and don't feel they negatively affect you, then you don't need to bother with any of this.

So, what did I do in this situation? When in doubt, go for compassion.

I began to think, "What could be going on in this guy's life that he can't make it through 30 minutes of meditation without falling asleep? I thought, "Wow, he must be really tired." Then I thought that his life at home must be so unrelaxed, that in meditation he nods immediately from the relief.

Then I considered that his snoring wasn't so bad (although I wasn't sitting next to him), and maybe it was slightly relaxing in a weird way. Then I realized his snoring was not such an imposing obstacle to my meditation and decided to practice rising above it.

There you have it. Get lost judge and victim. I don't need you upping my blood pressure, messing with my happy hormones, and lowering my pH.

One thing I absolutely know is that one's state of mind is as important, if not more important than physical contributors, to one's health.

Ain't no friggin judge and victim gonna mess with me!

Chapter 7

Make the Holidays Work for You

> *"Just as a puppy can be more of a challenge than a gift, so too can the holidays."* - John Clayton

When I was a kid, the holidays were a much simpler proposition. Everyone said "Merry Christmas," people sent cards that didn't have elaborate portraits of family, children, and pets. There were parties, and most people probably drove drunk at one point or another.

The store's Christmas decorations weren't up at Halloween, and you didn't have to worry about "Black Friday" or "Cyber Monday" shopping deals. You went out to the stores, bought some stuff, had it wrapped there or did it yourself, and gave it away. Yes, it was still a commercial proposition, but not to the astounding degree of today.

As with all aspects of shoving consumables down the throats of consumers, the holiday season is now all about the "holiday sales" season. It has been fine-tuned through studies in psychology, demographics, weather, economy, political party, and I'm sure much, much more.

It has become the 'science of maximum return' to be squeezed from people celebrating the birth of their religion's main guy, or from those celebrating the oil lamps that burned miraculously.

This can be a great time of year for some, yet very stressful for others.

Whatever direction it takes you, is largely determined by how willing you are to assert your will and intention on the experience.

Like so many things in life it seems much easier just to let ourselves be led through a process. Whether it be allowing our employer to define our worth, giving our health care over to someone, or allowing ourselves to be pushed along through the holidays, we subconsciously seek the path of least resistance.

Be it by habit, training, tradition, or media exposure, our impulse is to sit back and let some external force paint the picture of our life. Then we complain if it sucks, or we are happy if it's good.

If the result works for you, sit back and enjoy! If it's not working out, and you don't want to do anything about it, don't complain! However, if it's not working, and you do something about it, good for you! Because you see, the holidays can be thought of as a microcosm version of your life.

Life, like the holidays, can give you stress, joy, and all the other emotional states. The degree to which you can make this manufactured process of reality (aka the holidays) operate in your favor, is probably indicative of *how capable you are to make other aspects of your life work in your favor.*

You may want to try practicing your life management skills during the holidays. It is a perfect opportunity to exercise your powers of intention, will, manifestation, patience, and discipline.

It's all there - a life laboratory experiment just waiting for you. Consider this as food for thought, spiritual food, not holiday food!

There are some excellent non-monetary assets that can be garnered during the holidays as well. Spiritual perks can be gained through the use of "collective consciousness."

The power of group focus cannot be underestimated, and it doesn't even have to be a large group. In the Bhagavad Gita, Krishna tells us, "Anytime two or more gather in my name, I am there." If we take advantage of religious holidays, regardless of our spiritual leanings, our experience can be enhanced.

I love my meditations on Sunday mornings, Easter, Christmas, Passover, and the Indian holidays honoring the different Hindu deities. It doesn't matter that I may not be of the same religion. It only matters that for those relatively short periods of time, a greater percentage of the population is tuned in a little more toward the spiritual, and a little less toward the material. In this world, every bit helps.

I hope you find a way to bring meaning and joy into your life on a daily basis, and not just on special occasions.

You have the ability to paint the life you want on the canvas of reality. It's right in front of you. But you have to pick up the brush.

Chapter 8

Your Life and the Collective Karma

> *"You are free to choose, but you are not free from the consequence of your choice."- Anonymous*

There I sat, on the eve of the holiday, pondering the birth of one of the great spiritual leaders of this planet's current history. As the story goes, a poor boy born in a manger surrounded by farm animals. A message of "peace on earth and goodwill toward men."

How many centuries have passed, and must pass, before we get that right? Evidently a lot.

This creation is dreams within dreams; the dreams of individuals, families, groups, societies, and humankind as a whole. Each with its own personal or collective input and manifestation. This ever-changing temporary reality is responding to the consciousness being directed at it.

You don't even have to be a new age thinker to embrace that concept. Quantum physics and neuroscience will back you up.

All this collective thought is creating our world. But we also have collective karma affecting outcomes. Cause and effect in play. So, with that said, is there really any reason to expect any other result than the hate-mongering, fear-driven, war-ridden situation in which we live?

Our collective behavior does nothing to bring anything other than negative karmic results to the big dream we are living. Let's look at how we treat our home. We pollute the ocean and rape, strip mine, clear-cut, and frack the land. Big corporations, governments, and leaders are willing to sacrifice millions of lives, human and animal, for the sake of profit and personal gain.

And, to me, the most appalling and disgusting aspect of human behavior is the torture and abuse of children and the gentle creatures who share this planet with us.

If someone guilty of those crimes was brought to trial, would you expect, or want, the judge to say, "Well no worries, we will just make your life better and better, forever and ever?" Of course not, and yet that is what we seem to think should be happening to us.

The stark results of the condition of our world would suggest that Nature and karma do not agree with that.

We are fortunate, indeed, to have been born into the life we have. But this does not exonerate us from a responsibility to the greater good. We hopefully wouldn't say, "Well I got a good seat on the bus, so I'm cool, tough luck for everyone else." But without thinking, that is exactly what we sometimes do.

We are so wrapped up in our personal dream existence, and we assume it doesn't matter to the big picture, but it does.

It is not popular to point this stuff out. Everyone wants rainbows and unicorns and "positive energy." But karma does not respond to energy, it responds to action. Action is the exact translation of the Sanskrit word, "karma."

We have all heard the saying that the definition of insanity is repeating the same thing over and over with the expectation of a different result. Yet that is exactly what we do.

Most people show up, in exactly the same way, every day and think that somehow things will suddenly get better. That just doesn't seem to be working.

We all need to be active. Find a cause, something that matters to you. Find something you are passionate about, something that contributes to making the planet better. *Give your time or give your money, but give something. It matters.*

It has been said, "If you aren't part of the solution, you are part of the problem." I wish it weren't so, but the truth of it is we cannot exploit life just for our own happiness without concern for the greater good of the tribe.

By caring for that greater good, you might be surprised by what you receive: returns of purpose, satisfaction, and karmic reward.

Wouldn't it be amazing, instead of just having a new year, to have a new kind of year? One that moved towards peace on earth...and goodwill toward humankind?

Chapter 9

David Bowie. The Visionary Personality

> *"The measure of intelligence is the ability to change." - Albert Einstein*

I just watched a video of David Bowie, perfectly predicting the ramifications of the internet on music, art, and society in the year 1999! This, in itself, is amazing, but what makes it even more interesting is the responses by the interviewer, Jeremy Paxman.

He is apparently, while of a similar age to Bowie, of an entirely different and far more conservative culture. What makes this interesting, is his views and comments on what Bowie has to say.

Paxman downplays the importance of the internet saying it is only a "tool," "a different delivery system," and he feels claims being made for it (the internet) are "hugely overrated."

This is coming from someone who makes his living in media! Bowie doesn't back down for a minute, and says "What the internet is going to do to society is unimaginable."

As Bowie is a visionary in his art, he is a visionary in other things as well. What does this have to do with us and our lives? We should take a serious look at ourselves and ask, "Am I a "Bowie" or a "Paxman?" The answer is not as obvious as we would like to think.

One of the more telling things, to me, in this interview is at the beginning when Bowie talks about his reasons for becoming a musician.

He talks about the attraction of the rebellious nature of Rock music at that time. He talks about the difficulty in finding sources of music to listen to. He talks about how the music had a "call to arms kind of feeling to it" and an opportunity to "affect change."

These are the thoughts, feelings, and words of someone who is attracted to, and comfortable with, the idea of being uncomfortable. This is the mindset of people who generate change and progress at any level.

Because in the process of living in that reality, you will at least on occasion, be subjected to discomfort by the Paxmans of the world. To this, I speak from personal experience.

We, the creatures of this reality, are programmed to survive. This programmed survival operates in an entirely reactive manner. One of its primary reactions is to run from or fight danger and to move toward and seek comfort in safe familiarity. Or, as the yogis would simply put it, "Seek pleasure and avoid pain."

What this means is that we tend to observe unfamiliar circumstances around us with bias towards suspicion. This is natural because we are accessing danger. All of this works great when we are dealing with ferocious wild animals, and safe caves, but becomes more confused with modern living and relationships.

The considerations of Paxman come from the comfort, familiarity and success he enjoys from things as they are. *Any potential change to this familiar environment threatens his comfort, and he reacts with suspicion and rejection.*

Bowie, on the other hand, has lived the life of an artist. He knows the insecurity and tenuous nature of succeeding in popular culture. He understands "ch, ch, ch, changes... Turn and face the strange."

Those words! Are you friggin kidding me? Amazing!

Unfortunately for the Paxmans of the world, the model has changed. The speed at which information, news, ideas and opinion travel is rapidly encroaching on the luxury of "comfortable complacency."

We will all look at this, and no doubt say, "Oh yeah, I'm definitely a Bowie. I'm hip. I'm on Facebook, Instagram and Twitter, I'm into technology, and I do yoga." Sorry, 'fraid not.

It has nothing to do with any of that. This is about our actual ability to be outside of our comfortable preconceptions of our environment, other people, other cultures, different economic models and so much more. What does all that have to do with seeing the future?

Because, as Paxman proves here, if we can't see outside our comfortable preconceptions or perceptions, we cannot see *Potential.*

Our state of whatever mental fluidity and adaptability we have is a result of our acquired beliefs. Beliefs acquired mostly, at the hands of adults, when we were children.

These mental states and processes are not written in stone. There are many methods we can apply, both self-help and assisted, to change our beliefs and behavior.

That, of course, requires most importantly the desire to make any changes. Then it takes the work and application of the methods.

As a side note, and without getting into personal opinions of politics, I will say this. Generally speaking, all the people we are offered as choices at the polls, to operate our government, have high levels of comfort and success associated with the existing paradigm.

We are highly unlikely to see any visionary change from them or the system they operate within. They are the "Paxmans" of the world.

So, you have the choice of living your life as a Bowie or a Paxman.

I feel that the great value of visionary people is not only owing to what they give us as knowledge, art, or technology, but also in the example of their capacity to see and imagine possibilities.

Rest in Peace David, and thank you for your genius and vision!

Chapter 10

Life Lessons from John Travolta

> *"Success and charisma often go
> hand in hand" - DD*

When I was a fair bit younger and had gotten my start in the movie business, I worked on a movie called "Face Off." The film starred John Travolta and Nicolas Cage.

Now, this was not the John Travolta of today. The one who has endured a few justly deserved, and not so justly deserved, embarrassments and humiliations.

I had never met John, and I remember the first time I saw him on set. You must remember, that this was around 1997. He was experiencing an amazing comeback that included" Get Shorty" and "Pulp Fiction."

I am not easily star-struck, but having grown up with his presence on television and in films, I noticed the effortless charisma that he possessed.

As I watched him walk through the set, I wondered if he is who and where he is because of this charisma, or if he possesses this charisma because this is what he has become?

Some 20 years later, I think I have figured it out. His charisma was not something he was necessarily born with, nor was it a product of what he had become. It was, however, a byproduct of his mindset.

That mindset was that he had a *true and devoted mission in life.* The mission to succeed in the first place, and the mission to succeed in his comeback.

And now I have a better understanding of how this focused mindset of having a mission affects the charisma and magnetism of individuals. And, also as is the case with some, why further into their career, these qualities diminish.

This is also something I have observed in some of the rock bands I have enjoyed through the years. They burst onto the scene with power, energy, and charisma only to fall into obscurity after a few hit records.

And let us make no mistake about it. There is a significant difference between a mission and an aspiration, desire, or interest. The mission is all-consuming.

So, what are the traits people display when having this purpose or mission in life, that generate this charisma and magnetism? Here are few:

- They don't have time for the distractions of petty drama and time-wasting bullshit. They are willing to ignore or evict people who bring that into their life. The focus of their mission does not have space for such trivial distractions.

- They are not emotionally needy when it comes to other people. The needs and demands of accomplishing their mission exclude constant dependence on other people. This is not to say that they won't need others in the pursuit of their mission. However, these interactions should be conducted with discipline and intellect, not emotional dependency.

- They are not needy financially. Being needy financially too often puts people in a position of subservience and compromise. There is no room for these negative traits in the people working towards great outcomes. This is not to say you need to be financially independent to attain your goal. It means that the source of your income should be reliable, not highly stressful, and leave you the time and opportunity to pursue the mission.

- They don't care about the opinion of others. There is an old saying, "Lions don't lose sleep over the opinions of sheep." You will never please everyone, and usually, when you piss off or offend someone, it is more about their shortcomings and insecurities than your own.

These qualities and characteristics naturally create a mystique in these people which makes them attractive to others. Without consciously trying, they project to the world an air of interest in things above and beyond the mundane preoccupations of most people.

It is a strange paradox in life that people are often attracted to people whom they find attractive, but who have no interest in them. This is not to say that people with a mission have a license to be unkind or abusive to others. Their indifference is just a byproduct of their preoccupation with the task at hand.

It seems this attraction to the unattainable is often apparent in our societies' fixation on celebrities who possess wealth, fame and talent. Because of the media's constant spotlight on all that they do, people feel they know these famous people on a personal level. And yet the celebrities, with whom they feel a connection, have no knowledge or connection to them at all and are in fact entirely beyond their reach.

And many fans become obsessively attached. Now, of course, if the fan had an actual mission of their own, they would not have time or interest for such pathetic behavior.

Lastly, while not related to personality traits, there is a quality that separates a more mundane or ordinary aspiration from one with more far-reaching effects. And that is the size of the mission's impact.

Let's have a look at parenthood. There are many mothers, out there, who would read this and say, "of course I have a mission, and that is to raise my child to be the best person that they can be." This is a very valuable and necessary aspiration.

The problem is, with over seven billion humans on this earth, the impact of their mission is not particularly unusual or far-reaching. This is not to say that it is not a highly valuable and necessary task. It is just to say that outside of your family or close circle of friends, it probably has no effect or interest to most of the world.

Finding cures for disease, creating beneficial technology, starting a business or writing a best-selling book, creating a hit song or a fantastic app could have a far greater impact on a far greater number of people.

I can hear the cries of the mothers now, "What about Barack Obama's mother?" What about that mission?" And to that, I say, "What about Hitler's mother?" The outcome of the child's mission, be it to become president or conquer the world, is not the same as the parent's mission in raising the child.

Anyone who thinks the outcome of a child's life is all about their upbringing has never seen twins, or two siblings less than two years apart in age, raised in the same environment by the same parents, and the differences between them. Everyone comes into this world with a package of their own.

Ultimately, for many people, when the success of the mission has been realized the qualities possessed during the pursuit of the mission fade away.

This often has to do with how open-ended the mission was initially.
.
If the endgame of the mission is definite and well-defined, and success is achieved, it is natural for the person to relax and become comfortable in their success. This is as it should be. The Intensity required in pursuing an all-

consuming mission is not an easy thing to sustain.

It is at this point many fall into enjoying their success and have time to re-engage with the more superficial aspects of life. This, of course, diminishes the charismatic and focused personality traits they possessed in their original pursuits.

This is noticeable when we see some celebrities and artists who, after having achieved success, somehow appear more complacent, more common, and less fascinating.

I'm not saying one is right or one is wrong. I am also not saying that an all-consuming mission is necessary for a complete or happy life.

But I can say from personal experience that during periods of my life when I have had an all-consuming mission, it has had an interesting effect on how I've viewed or was affected by life events. The drama involving family and friends, affairs of the heart, or work issues just seemed less intense and bothersome.

At times, I was accused of being cold, detached, or unemotional. That was not the case at all. I was just preoccupied with the mission.

There is a point, and possible action, to all of this and here it is:

If the everyday events of life are causing you distress, anxiety, or depression maybe what you need rather than therapy, antidepressants, or complaining to your friends is a badass mission of your own.

Chapter 11

A Friend in Need

> *"A human being is part of a whole, called by us the 'Universe."* - *Albert Einstein*

Sometimes, like many people, I feel sad or depressed. I may aimlessly go online to social media and look at what my "friends" are up to. It is usually the same thing; superficial events presented in a way that indicates that things are good. Either that or social justice and political opinions being freely dispensed.

Sometimes I think "Who could I call to talk about things." Many of my better friends are spread out in different places. I can't see them in person, and even communication can be a challenge. And then I go down the list. This one is super busy. This one is out of town. Another is going through her own heavy stuff, and I haven't talked to this one in so long. Lots of friends and contacts, but no one to talk to. It wasn't always like that.

Long ago in a place not so far away:

I sat on the beach—18 years old and heartbroken.

It was a classic case of teen love ending in teen angst. My girlfriend, at the time had been drifting into into other things and other friends was acting disconnected and distant. We had been together earlier that day, and maybe I felt the premonition of things to come.

We needed to have "the talk." I was young and inexperienced, and I'm not sure how or why, but at that moment, I sort of blurted out, *"I like you—and I love you."*

It was the first time in my short—and obviously not cool—life that I had professed my love to anyone. Her reply was so perfect in its pure, unaffected, brutal harshness. She said, *"I know, but we can't stay together. I'm having too much fun."*

That was my introduction to love. As I've gone through life, I have heard of some bad results from telling someone you love them—but I'm not sure any were worse than that.

I did the only thing I could do at a time like that—I went to the beach because I knew I would find my friends there. It was where we surfed and hung out, and our lives revolved around it. It was our place.

It was a different time. There were no cell phones, email or texting. We were a group. Not the group that you find yourself with at work, or school, or on "the team." We were just a group of boys who happened to came together through circumstance and cosmic attraction.

Each person's life and reality contributed to the total experience of the collective group. *We were a tribe.* We were so close that it was as if there was little separation between our individual lives and our shared path together.

There was no virtual communication. We made our plans for tomorrow in person today. It was organic, real and never affected by the confusion of a strange or uncertain text or email.

I sat on the beach, looking at the water, listening to the sound of the waves, and hoping the ocean could calm my pain.

My friend sat down beside me on the sand. He was not the most reliable friend—not the one I would call if I were in trouble. But it was okay because that is the thing about a tribe—each member has something of value to add. The sum of the parts becomes greater than any individual.

He knew that there was something wrong, but he just sat and said nothing. Probably picked up a twig and doodled in the sand or flipped some of the little shells. After a while, he said,

"*What's up?*" So, I told him, leaving out the embarrassing part about telling her that I loved her. I've never forgotten what followed.

His perfect response was so authentic and unaffected by any kind of contrived sympathy. He said with complete and utter spontaneous belief and conviction, "*I always thought you could do better anyway.*"

Now, I know that is something that people often say to appease broken hearts, but this was different. Maybe it was our age. Perhaps it was our connection and influence on each other— but *it would never have had the same effect by phone, text, email or with someone I only saw rarely.*

Without thought, I surrendered to his personal conviction and sincerity. In that moment, I *saw and felt* his truth.

A calm relief came over me. I was still hurting, but it was much better. I didn't say anything, and we sat for a while looking at the ocean. Then he spoke the second perfect thing, asking "*Want to go surf down south tomorrow?*" "*Okay,*" I said.

My tribe had taken care of me.

We live in a much different situation today. We interact with our tribe through electronic communication.

We are exposed to a much larger group that we are much less close to. We know personal information about what is happening with people we wouldn't even see or talk to if it weren't for social media.

Many of us have quantity rather than quality, and information rather than communication in our connections.

We don't need to interact, with people we know, for many things. We can go online and have someone we don't know refer us to a service by someone we don't know. It's all very convenient, and it gives us a great sense of independence and power.

That's the illusion because we are still relying on someone else. The virtual nature just de-personalizes it.

Our relationship with our tribe is now very controllable. We have the inherent flaws of technology to protect our lack of interest or commitment. We can all say, *"I had a problem with my phone this afternoon."* We can cherry pick the information we give our group on social media.

Then we wonder—in the moments when our humanity rears its head—why we feel disconnected and hollow.

Words constitute only a small percentage of actual communication. The tone of voice, body language, and energy are a huge aspect of it, and we are losing this. This is the life technology has given us. It is like a Twinkie. It is real, but not organic, and it may not be healthy.

Technology and social media are hugely valuable tools for—among other things—disseminating information and giving a voice to grassroots causes. But they should not replace the human experience. This life is nothing without its lessons in human connection.

This is the testing ground of our ability to step outside of ourselves and surrender our ego and bias. To be who we are in the flesh and not filtered through a screen. To find our way into love and compassion, and out of hate and prejudice. *To see our oneness with all living things.*

I want to see people—hug them and shake their hands. I want to look them in the eyes and *feel their spirit and presence.*

It matters a lot—because, with the right intention, this connection with our tribe is the prelude to an understanding of ourselves and our connection to all creation. And that is an experience worth pursuing.

Part Two
Yoga

Chapter 12

Yoga
The Arsenal

> *Yoga as a Weapon in the War on Suffering.*

There are those, of the rainbows, unicorns, and positive energy, school of thought, who may find the analogy of war and battle to life unbecoming. However, mouthing words like "love and light" while practicing the opposite behavior of living in narcissism and self-indulgent drama is a very common activity these days.

But, lest there be any confusion, the Bhagavad Gita, considered by many to be the definitive discourse on yoga, takes place on a battlefield. And not just any battlefield. It is on the plains of Kurukshetra, on the eve of the greatest war the world and humanity have ever known - a war that will change the world forever.

My words on the Gita, as it is often and affectionately referred to for short, are for another book.

All I wish to convey here is that, ultimately, yoga is a discipline aimed at subduing and hopefully eliminating the suffering of the individual.

And make no mistake, it is a battle. A battle for supremacy that is constantly being waged between the light and love of soul and spirit, and the darkness and fear of the mind, ego, and senses.

While I have chosen cancer as the opponent/enemy subject of this book, there are many others. Addiction, sickness, depression, and physical injury are just a few of many enemies we could face in our lifetime. The forms of potential suffering dealt out so freely in this existence, are beyond measure.

Yoga was designed and meant to be a remedy, or weapon if you will, against that suffering.

Chapter 13

Yoga and Asana

> *"Yoga teaches us to cure what need not be endured and endure what cannot be cured."-*
> *BKS Iyengar-*

Before we begin this journey into yoga, I must address a primary understanding, or misunderstanding, of what most people consider to be yoga.

Today most people take it for granted that yoga is a form of exercise of which there are several different styles and methods. This is true of one aspect of yoga that I generally refer to as "Hatha" Yoga.

This can be slightly confusing in that some people consider "Hatha" yoga to be a particular style of physical practice. In addition to that, there are other physical practices within Hatha yoga systems that extend beyond doing postures (asanas).

So, if I refer to "hatha" from here on, I am only referring to the practice of the physical postures. I will also refer to it as "asana" as in that part of Hatha yoga which is the "asana" practice.

The Sanskrit word asana translates to "seat" and was probably designated originally, by the Indian sage Patanjali, as a comfortable and effective seated position in which to meditate. It has since been adapted to mean "pose" or "posture" when applied to the different physical yoga poses.

This matters because as we move further into this subject, it will become clear that "asana" isn't the totality of yoga. In fact, yoga can exist entirely without asana, and asana can exist entirely without yoga. As I said, this will become clear as we progress.

There is also a considerable difference between a "Yogi" (someone who practices the totality of yoga) and someone who "does yoga" (meaning someone who does yoga postures, either on their own or in classes, as a form of physical exercise.}

The Value of Asana

The value of asana, as related to health, is its amazing and effective form of maintaining physical well-being. It can be done at many different levels of exertion, from completely relaxed and restorative to extremely vigorous and challenging.

This makes it an ideal form of exercise for anyone, regardless of age, gender, physical condition or health. There are very few people, in any given situation, who cannot benefit from asana practice.

Many people think asana is limited to and requires flexibility. This is not true. There is a common saying these days that goes like this, "Saying you aren't flexible enough to do yoga is like saying you are too dirty to take a shower."

It isn't how flexible you are. It's about opening up your body from wherever you are today. Your practice will probably never look like the gymnast/dancer in the front row of the class, and that is totally ok.

I am a Believer

Yoga postures are designed and intended to be beneficial on many levels. Increasing flexibility, from whatever place you begin, is only one benefit. The postures contribute to helping balance the nervous system, improving breathing, increasing focus, enhance relaxation and more. This is the reason that asana has become so popular.

I have practiced asana for over 40 years and taught it for 20. Many, many other physical pastimes have come in and out of my life, but I have always done asana or at least some form of stretching and breathing throughout it all. To say I am a great proponent of the practice would be an understatement.

I am not entirely happy with the state of yoga asana these days. Far too much emphasis is being placed on physical/acrobatic accomplishment. It is also being taught by too many people with not enough experience. This is resulting in too much physical injury as well as too much ego attachment to the practice.

I believe that at no time, during the asana practice, should a person experience unpleasant levels of pain or discomfort. Pursuing, with force, a posture that results in any long-term compromising injury is not acceptable.

I will go deeper into this as we move ahead, but I want something to be very clear. While I consider the most valuable aspects of yoga to exist outside of asana, the asana practice has a very useful position in anyone's life.

Chapter 14

What and Why is Yoga?

"Yoga is the journey of the self, through the self, to the self." - The Bhagavad Gita

I thought it would be best to begin this section on yoga talking about exactly what yoga is, and for that matter, why it is.

Most people today practice yoga as a form of exercise, without understanding what it's deeper aspects are, and why it exists.

This is entirely understandable given the fact that yoga has been primarily offered to the public as a form of exercise. The exercise aspect of the asanas (or postures) is a legitimate part of a yoga practice. However, it is not the aim of yoga or even an essential part of a yoga practice.

On the spiritual level, yoga is not a religion. *Yoga is a science.*

If you've been around yoga much, or taken a teacher training, you have probably heard that the word "yoga" comes from the Sanskrit root word "yuj" which means to "yoke" or "unite."

In the past, when teachers used to address this, they would have some socially generic version of "yoga is a union of body and mind" or "union of body, mind and soul" But there is one big issue with this. The body, mind, and soul are already united, and therein lies the problem.

I can imagine the disbelief! How could anything so beautiful be a problem! Bear with me, my friends, all will be revealed.

Now we will take a trip down memory lane.

Yoga (not asana) was developed, long ago. in a more enlightened age. This is obvious when we look back at the evidence of great civilizations of the past, and compare them to the dark ages we were in a thousand years ago. It would appear that we went from something better to something worse.

Now we are coming out of the dark age, as can be seen by our recent discoveries in many different fields.

This is in accordance with the yoga science of the "cycles of ages" or "yugas" that says we are emerging from the Kali Yuga (a dark and ignorant age) and moving into more enlightened times.

Within different philosophies and schools, the cycles are interpreted differently, and many people/scholars may want to take issue with my statement. To them, I can only say this. I follow my teacher's school of interpretation, and if they have a problem with it, take it up with Self Realization Fellowship, and Swami Sri Yukteshwar. (Although to have a direct conversation with him they will, indeed, need to be enlightened masters).

At any rate, back in those times of higher consciousness and understanding, the ancient yogis realized that the mechanics of material creation (life as we know it) brought certain aspects of suffering. So, they set about to find a remedy for suffering: physical, mental and spiritual suffering

Let's refer back to the above mentioned, inaccurate definition of yoga. "A union of body, mind, and soul" Well, that is where the ancients found the problem. The union or "connection" of the limiting nature of the body and mind (and associated ego) are messing things up, especially for the soul.

What they realized was that the answer to the problem was in connecting (yoga, to yoke or connect) the individual soul with the collective spirit, thus bypassing the difficulties and entanglements of the body and mind.

We will now quantify "soul" and "spirit" because these can easily be confused.

While the soul is indeed spirit, it is that small piece of temporarily individualized spirit that identifies you. It is like a wave in the ocean. It is of the same substance and an integrated part of the ocean but, not the entire ocean.

Spirit is the fabric within and outside of creation. The entire ocean, if you will. You can call it God or Goddess, The Force, or Cosmic Intelligence, Allah, Jehovah, or the quantum field. You can fight wars over the names, sacrifice life, worship it, or deny it, and it won't make one bit of difference. You are in it, and part of it, no matter how much your little ego resists or embraces the idea.

So, "yoga" is essentially a disconnection of the individual soul from the body and mind, and the "yuj" or connection of yoga, is of the soul with spirit.

In that state, the soul is given a view of true reality. The little wave can experience the perception of the vast ocean. It then can have a better understanding of its true nature, capabilities, capacity for love and bliss, and perception beyond the confines of this limited, and soul-stifling, existence.

You will hear this theme repeated on occasion throughout this book. It is not that I don't have enough words to fill the pages or think you are not smart.

It is simply that learning of this kind is more often being reminded of something that we already know, rather than the acquisition of something new.

And truth bears repeating.

Chapter 15

A Husky and the Path to End Suffering. Part 1

> *"Though our conduct seems so very different from that of the higher animals, the primary instincts are much alike in them and in us."* - *Albert Einstein*

I had a Siberian Husky once. It's funny, but you will often hear that from people who have had a Husky. Rarely will you ever hear, "I've had a few Huskies," or "My family always had huskies." One Husky is usually enough for most people.

They are very high-maintenance dogs. They are independent and willful and are the most closely related to wolves of the domestic dogs. They love nothing more than to run or jog (since pulling sleds is the job for which they were used for generations). They tend to be non-aggressive toward humans and other dogs, probably because being used in group situations (as in sled teams), individual dogs that exhibited aggressive behavior were destroyed.

They also are born hunters. Since the ability to find some food on their own was not considered a bad thing, it was not discouraged.

When "Jack," my Husky, was less than a year-old, I was riding my bike with him in an unpopulated area, and he was off the leash.

We were on a single-track dirt path. We rounded a little corner and came upon a rabbit in the path. The rabbit bolted, Jack went after it. In about 10 seconds the rabbit was dead, and being dropped at my feet as a contribution to the pack. It was all very matter-of-fact.

He didn't seem proud of himself and certainly didn't seem worried that he had done anything wrong. It was as if it were business as usual, and he seemed more interested in continuing our walk.

He had come to me as a puppy from a shelter. He had been taken, by animal control, from an idiot owner who had a litter of pups and was neglecting them. The point is he had never been in the wild or had a parent teach him how to hunt, nor had he seen it done before.

It struck me that I had witnessed a purely instinctive reaction. It was so pure in its intention, focus, method, and execution. It was a product, as were so many of his traits, of generations of survival of his species, combined with breeding, and repeated specific work his breed had performed.

For him to have become something other than what he was would probably have been improbable, if not impossible. It was imprinted in his DNA, essentially, in every cell of his body.

Interesting story, right? But, of course, it leads us into aspects of introspection and self-assessment.

It's Not about the Thumbs

As humans, we love to think of ourselves as very special, both individually and collectively. We like to believe our "superior cognitive intellect," and opposable thumb has made us so special that other species and even our environment are servants and hosts to our voracious appetites and "superior" needs and wants.

Actually, it is not our intellect or thumbs that makes us so (wrongfully) confident of our superiority...It is our ego.

No matter what is going on in our mind, if we are in a body, we are a carbon-based life form. The survival reactions, skills, and traits we exhibit in that life form are no different from the Husky. We are linked in so many ways, as individuals and as a group, to the experiences of our predecessors, in every cell of our bodies.

We usually don't see it unless it's something we are proud of. Then our ego likes It. As in, "Yeah, my dad is an amazing musician, that's where I got it from."

The ego does not contribute to intelligence or cognitive thought. It only provides reactive thought response to events that either reaffirm or threaten its sense of separateness or individuality.

The ego's impulse to separate is like a loaded gun – not inherently dangerous by itself, but brutal when misused.

Generally, the ego will do everything in its power to maintain separateness. That is its primary function. It does not want to admit that we are in any way connected to or influenced by our instincts, DNA, or, most importantly, our true spiritual nature.

Its motivation for this closed-minded line of thinking is fear. The ego is always operating from a place of fear whereas love, compassion, and feelings of unity manifest from the spiritual part of our diverse consciousness.

Why would anyone want to be influenced by such a limiting and self-serving proposition as ego-based fearful thinking?

Because without it we could not play on this playing field of material creation.

It allows us to act as individuals. Without it, we would exist in a state of constant unity with our environment, and all the living things around us.

Everything We Do Comes at a Price

The ego comes with dangerous traits that allow us to play the game. You may say, "Why would God (or whatever name you choose) do that?" Because with everything that happens in material creation, no matter what it is, there will always be good and bad, light and dark, love and fear, generosity and greed and the list goes on.

Opposites, or "duality" are a law of this universe.

If you want to surf, you may drown. That is the risk you take. Want to play football? You may get a concussion or blow out a knee - it is a risk you take. Want to drive to the store for groceries? You could get in a car accident and die. That is the risk you take.

Want to play as a human on Earth? The ego, which comes with that experience, could dominate your thinking and lead you to suffer. That is the risk you take.

What do we do? If we want to surf, we learn how to swim well to reduce our risk of drowning. Play football? Make sure we wear the best protective gear possible. Drive to the store? Become the best driver we can.

Want to thrive despite the pitfalls of ego-based fear thinking? Most people don't do anything, and that is the problem.

They understand that there are physical dangers to avoid in life. That's easy. Physical pain is immediate and obvious. So they do what is, aside from the will to survive, the most fundamental of human behavior. They avoid pain to the best of their ability and pursue pleasure.

We Don't Address What We Don't See

Since we don't know that playing this game comes with inherent, but *preventable* psychological dangers, we accept emotional pain as normal, and uncontrollable. It is the "default" model.

So, what happens? Well, if our upbringing and environment were such that we had good examples and role models to emulate, we may do well with an outlook that embraces happiness, accepts diversity, and avoids fear-based thinking.

If not, we may live in conflict, antagonizing family and friends with drama, hurtful remarks and isolated, fearful thinking. Or we may go on the internet to lash out with opinions and comments to strangers. Or maybe worse, we adopt self-destructive behavior.

All this behavior is fear based ego acting out to reaffirm its delusive ideas of a superior, individual, identity.

What is the remedy to all this? In the next chapter, part 2, we will break it down.

Chapter 16

A Husky and the Path to End Suffering. Part 2

> *"The wolf changes his coat, but not his disposition."* -Proverb

In part 1 we have established that for us to partake in this game of life, in the material world, we need an ego. The ego maintains the separateness required for us to operate as individuals. When, where, and why we agreed to this dream delusion is unknown and perplexing to me.

I would like to see a record of the conversation that transpired where I decided living in this drama would be better than existing in a state of never-ending, ever-changing bliss, and connection to all things at the spiritual level.

But anyway, here we are and what are we going to do? Remember that the ego, like surfing, football, and driving, comes with inherent dangers.

In the same way that we would acquire protective equipment for football, or work on swimming skills for surfing, we must actively learn about and pursue methods to allow our higher soul/spirit consciousness to rise above ego thinking.

Take a Vacation from the Ego

Since what we have here is a predominance of ego influence, the obvious remedy is to move into a different frame of reference. Here is what we have:

This is the package from which most people operate: body/mind/ego connection.

These three are very involved with each other and are not easily separated; it works like this:

- We experience our reality through our senses (the body)
- The ego evaluates the experience and reacts to it. This is, usually, with a pre-programmed habit response based on protecting its individuality, and based on past experience. This mechanical response bypasses, and spares, cognitive effort.
- The mind then initiates thoughts and emotions around the ego reaction, usually based on nothing more than habit.

The Spirit is suppressed in all this because it is hypnotized by material creation. Its true cognitive awareness would shatter the illusion and threaten the ego's existence.

Spiritual Connection is the Key

Spirit exists both within and outside of material creation. This world and its workings are nothing more than a dream illusion of Spirit.

By definition, the qualities of Spirit are omnipresence and omnipotence. It is timeless, indestructible, and unchangeable. These qualities are not only reflected in greater aspects of vast spirit, but also in the souls of us all. When we can tap into and experience the reality of spirit, the ego's petty delusions are revealed.

Meditation is the Path, and Patanjali tells us how.

Patanjali, an Indian Sage, put together a blueprint of sorts around the 2nd or 3rd century CE with his eight limbs of yoga. Yoga (to "yoke" or "connect") to Patanjali, is the process of "connecting" the individual soul to collective spirit. His method is this:

- Yama and

- Niyama – correct behavior. This is the moral/ethical code of behavior that would be like The Ten Commandments or the Precepts of Buddhism. The Yamas are the "thou shalt not" and relate to our relationship with others and the outer world. The Niyamas are the "thou shalt" and address personal practices that relate to our "inner world."

Without correct behavior, karma will hamper the person's progress.

- Asana – Asana, as defined by Patanjali has nothing to do with Hatha yoga. He defines it as the correct alignment of the spine while practicing the following remaining limbs.

- Pranayama – The Sanskrit translation of pranayama is life force (or Prana) control. While this is usually practiced with breathing exercises, the breathing is not an end in itself. The ultimate objective is to gain control of the life force.

- Pratyahara – Once we have some control of the prana, we want to withdraw it from the senses. By doing this, we can stop, or at least slow, the input from the body to the ego and mind.

- Dharana – Concentration. Without the distraction of sensory input, we work on focused concentration. Once there we turn our focus towards spirit.

- Dhyana – meditation -This, for some, is a point of contention. From the teachings of my Guru (Paramahansa Yogananda) only concentration directed toward spirit qualifies as meditation. Any other form of focused mental effort would be concentration, contemplation, reflection or something of that nature.

- Samadhi – Samadhi can take different forms as the connection manifests with varying qualities of spirit. This is the place of total connection between soul and spirit. The result is a state where there is no separation or distinction between the "knower" and the "known" or the "observer," and the "object observed." Only the spiritual qualities of love, bliss, and connection are experienced.

Sounds Good, How Do I Do it?

Meditation is the way. However, there is no one way to meditate. Meditation requires a method and commitment to the practice. For some, a Buddhist meditation may work best. For some TM may work. For others Self Realization Fellowship techniques may be best. There are many styles and schools of meditation practice.

This is not an easy thing. Like any other-long term relationship in this world. First you must find the choice, and then commit to the choice.

Don't Get Lost in the "Flavor of the Month"

You may need to try different methods, hopefully when you are younger, to ultimately find your path.

As Westerners, our challenge is not to get lost chasing the variety and excitement of the "latest" thing. There is always some New Age guru with something new to sell you. You cannot bounce from one thing to another and make progress. Not in this game.

The stakes are too high, and the rewards too great. We are talking about freedom from suffering. That is a rare commodity in this reality and is not given easily.

People ask me, "How do you know when you've found your path?" At some point, hopefully, you will intuitively know that you have found something that resonates with you. It must be intuitive. This is not a job for intellect.

However, no effort or work that you put into this is wasted. Even if you decide to move on from one method to another, the work you have done is never in vain. Everything you do with the intention to draw closer to Spirit will have lasting effects

Hello Spirit, Goodbye Ego

As I said, what we are doing is taking a vacation from the ego. As we all know the physical environment we are immersed in will influence many things about us. That is why to make a change in our behavior, we often must make changes to our environment.

It is the same thing with our "internal" or mental/spiritual environment. We live in the body/mind/ego frame of reference so much of the time that many can't imagine there is anything else. But through meditation, we take our awareness into an entirely different paradigm.

Experiencing Spirit and Connection Rather than Ego and Separation

By using Patanjali's blueprint, and our meditation technique, we move away from our default body/mind/ego frame of reference and toward our true nature as spirit or soul.

Since spirit exists outside of material creation, our experience and attachment here are not subject to the "duality" of the material world. We are exposed to something that is more in line with who and what we truly are. Thus, the term "self-realization."

The more time we spend under the influence of the higher vibration of spiritual connection, the more we realize and are released from the suffering and relentless insecurity and fear of the ego.

And so, it is like "rehab" for the soul. We get away and "detox" from the corruption and pitfalls of this vehicle that we need for this physical experience.

We have provided the "protective equipment' and nurtured the skills necessary to make playing this game mentally and emotionally safer.

Consistency of practice is key

The ego does not just sit back and say, "Ok, you win, go ahead and enjoy your life as an ascended master." The ego is programmed for survival as well and has had much practice. Its methods of regaining its hold are subtle and effective.

It is essential to anchor ourselves in those higher states on a regular basis so as not to slip back into oblivious suffering. We need our viewpoint and automatic responses to be colored by our familiarity in self-realization and not in ego reactivity. Consistency of practice is key.

If these concepts and practices were simple to execute, this world would be a different place. People would feel happy, safe, and secure in their lives while feeling compassion and connection to all of creation. We are a helluva long way from that.

This is what defines and separates the "hardcore" from the "lightweight" or "wannabe" spiritual aspirant. The decision to undertake the pursuit of self-realization or soul actualization, and to follow through and apply it, is the realm of the true spiritual warrior.

Make no mistake, the reference to the warrior is not for dramatic effect. It is no coincidence that the lessons of yoga are taught to Arjuna by Krishna, in the Bhagavad Gita, are on the battlefield, on the eve of the greatest war the world would ever know. This path is a battle. It takes discipline, devotion and resolve.

What is the Reward?

I have a friend who has applied himself to the path. One-and-a-half to two-hour meditation every day, and sometimes more, for 20 years.

Recently he was dealing with having to find a new place to live and all the associated hassles.

I said to him, "Yeah it sucks having to go through all that stuff." He said to me, "It's ok...I just shut my eyes, and it's all gone."

To have the sanctuary of true reality, the reality that exists beyond this illusion. The reality of spiritual bliss and connection that knows no pain or suffering. That is the reward of the devoted spiritual aspirant.

Well Yeah, but...

One last point. You may look at this and say, "Well yeah, but escaping from this existence is just like taking drugs, and you still have to deal with it." This is typical ego fear thinking because it doesn't understand something very significant.

Here is the thing, and one of the most important points to remember. I can speak to this from first-hand experience. This is crucial. If you only take one thing from this, here it is...

The more time you spend with spirit and the more connection you build, the more spirit takes care of you.

This is an absolute spiritual truth and is summed up in what I think is the MOST important and relevant passage in the Bible:

"Seek ye first the kingdom of God (spirit), and all things shall be added unto you."

The world needs spiritual warriors now more than ever. Ego-based fear-aggression is very popular these days. It is apparent everywhere and disseminated through all forms of media.

Fear aggression is nothing special; animals express it all the time. The ego thinks it's "tough" and "hard-hitting." It is, in truth, weak, reactive and one-dimensional. It is for the punks and the bullies. It may look shiny and impressive, however, it is the path to division and suffering for us, as individuals and as a society. We need to do better than that!

Let Your Life Reflect Spirit and not Ego

Spend more time in the realm of spirit and truth.

Be an emissary of light. Be a warrior of truth and the highest qualities of Spirit. Seek and nurture your relationship with the source of all things, and that source will take care of you!

I honestly hope you find what it takes to rise above the ego and the mundane suffering of this world.

Chapter 17

When Asana Is Anti-Yoga

> *"It doesn't matter how deep into a posture you go. What matters is who you are when you get there." -Max Strom*

One time while riding in a car in India my friend asked the driver, "Do you practice yoga?" His reply was "My work is my yoga. I turn left, I turn right."

"Yoga" permeated his life. This is as it should be, and is how yoga is practiced in the culture that created it.

It is also the difference between "living the yoga," and "doing the yoga."

How many of us ask ourselves what exactly is yoga? How am I practicing yoga? What am I really doing here? It is very easy to fall into a kind of fixed relationship with yoga, and lose sight of what changes or opportunities our relationship with yoga may have to offer.

In modern, Western yoga that fixed relationship tends to revolve around the asana practice. How "good" are our postures, how deep we can go, or how good was our handstand today?

Here is an example of the irony of that thinking. I was asked by a swami I know, "How is your yoga?" My first thought was related to my asana practice and my teaching, and how that was going.

Then the truth dawned on me. He was not referring to the Hatha yoga practice at all. He was referring solely to my meditation practice.

Yoga, to him, has nothing to do with physical postures.

Understanding some of the fundamentals of what yoga is, and why it came about, opens the possibilities of what it offers. I have covered this in a previous chapter "What and Why is Yoga," if you care to reread it.

But to briefly refresh I will use this explanation from *The Complete Illustrated Book of Yoga* by Swami Vishnudevananda: "The aim of all yoga practice is to achieve truth wherein the individual soul identifies itself with (connects with) the supreme soul (spirit)."

And, as I stated before, this is done with the intention of alleviating suffering: physical, mental, and spiritual.

Then the soul can experience and realize its true natural state of bliss. Thus, the term "self-realization."

Now if that sounds to you like it doesn't have a lot to do with a handstand or a more "advanced posture," you would be correct.

Over 90 percent of the millions of people in India, along with our driver, who practice yoga don't do postures. They don't perceive a union with spirit as having anything to do with exercise.

There are different paths to the yoga connection. In the Bhagavad Gita, Krishna outlines three primary paths: Karma, Jnana, and Bhakti, or the yoga of action, knowledge, and devotion. They are not separate; they overlap.

As for "asana," as defined by Patanjali, it is strictly about posture and position of the spine while sitting during the practice of his "eight limbs of yoga."

You may be thinking, "But what about Hatha Yoga?" Generally, among more traditional practitioners, Hatha Yoga is considered support to the others and is not an end in itself.

So, where does the physical Hatha style of yoga that we see everywhere fit into all this?

- A clean and healthy body makes all the pursuits and responsibilities of life more manageable.
- It allows for more comfort while sitting for long periods of meditation.
- It gives us discipline that can spill over into other parts of life.
- It helps prana to move more efficiently in the body.
- It can help us connect with the breath.
- It can help detoxify the body, and of course, it can make us feel good.

That is the good news. Now for the bad.

The second of **Buddha's Four Noble Truths** tells us that "attachment is the source of all suffering." In the Bhagavad Gita, Krishna warns against attachment to the fruits (results) of one's actions.

If we pursue the yoga practice with ego-based attachment or pride, and I have been guilty of this, we are going in the opposite direction of yoga. *We are generating attachment.*

But the greatest irony to me, as a yoga teacher, is physical injury. I know that injury can occur. We can injure ourselves doing household chores. But how many people do we know who continuously injure themselves in their practice, in some ego/pride-based pursuit of accomplishment?

This is an attachment to a result at the expense of physical suffering.

Let me ask you something. If we are injuring ourselves practicing yoga, something created to alleviate suffering, are we truly practicing yoga?

There is nothing wrong with attempting a challenging physical endeavor that tests us, or even injures us, in our pursuit of imagined perfection and the resulting temporary happiness and satisfaction that it may bring.

But, if that is the case, it probably shouldn't be called "yoga."

The good thing is that since I live in LA, and spend so much time driving, maybe I can practice my yoga turning left and turning right.

Chapter 18

Choosing What Not to Do

> *"If you're not sure of what to do, first decide what not to do." - DD*

Having practiced Yoga for 40 years, and having taught for 20, I am still continually amazed at some of the choices people make on the mat. With that said, I find some of the most impressive practices resonating with the things people chose not to do.

I have the luxury and privilege of teaching some very accomplished practitioners, people with 20 years of experience and senior teachers. I know what they are capable of, and yet I see them removing all ego from the practice and allowing themselves the freedom and space to move through the perfect flow for them on that day. They stay in the breath and out of danger of injury.

Their practice varies day-to-day depending on what they are experiencing within themselves at that time. They are aware. To me, this is the epitome of an advanced yogi.

In less experienced students, the typical approach seems to be somewhat consistent. They tend to use a high level of effort and do the same difficult (and usually poorly aligned) version of the asana every time. Others just try for the most difficult version possible and, at some point or another, injure themselves with a fair amount of regularity.

The problem with this is that it shows an attachment to a physical "something." This quality is warned against, by both Buddha and Krishna, as a recipe for suffering and is not considered a good thing for anyone. It also displays a lack of body awareness and lack of respect for the body, both of which are key yoga fundamentals.

It is a sad statement in today's yoga that so much focus on "accomplishment" is based on strength, flexibility, and acrobatic prowess. If we feel the necessity to "measure" things, these are the last qualities by which a person's practice should be measured. Rather we should look at harmony, balance, awareness, respect, and gratitude on the mat. Are those not the traits we want in ourselves, and others, off the mat?

Practice with intention. Let the practice live and breathe in a safe, harmonious way. Release the bonds of ego attachment and find the real value of yoga. We have all heard the teacher say, "Honor your body." But it is more than that. It is honoring the practice and the concept of what yoga truly is.

Chapter 19

The Immersive Experience

"*Affirming and acknowledging your limitations only gives them strength.*" - DD

Like many people, when I travel, I always try to make my travels an immersive experience. I want to get an authentic feel for the place I am visiting.

When I was young and traveling, we called it "Groovin with the locals." We would try to find and experience the most authentic aspects of a place's culture, customs, and cuisine. Hey, a trinity all starting with "C." I like it!

The concept of the "immersive" experience is very prevalent these days. The wide-angle and ultra-portability of the GoPro camera is designed to put the viewer more "in the experience," and not as separated from it as in the traditional "spectator" point of view.

And, of course, the ultimate goal of "virtual reality" is to put the person squarely in the computer-generated events in which they are indulging.

This will allow unhealthy, out of shape guys to kill zombies, kick Chuck Norris's ass and get all the hot girls. All this while crumbs of nacho-flavored Doritos chips litter their shirts and couches. Can I say, "The Matrix, anyone?"

We like to flatter ourselves with our prowess at being able to adjust to foreign cultures we visit. We want to show our compassion and empathy for the culture, and not be the 'Ugly American" or "offensive" tourist. We pride ourselves on our ability to "immerse" ourselves in the experience. And we do pull it off occasionally, for brief moments.

But the problem is we can't really...because *our perception became more narrow and isolated as our ego matured and created its boundaries for us.*

I have heard, more than once, from various swamis and spiritual teachers, that the aim of spiritual enlightenment should manifest a more "childlike" frame of mind in the practitioner. A first impression of this concept may seem unrealistic to most people. After all, how could we function as adults with a childlike awareness?

First, let's establish some things. In a perfect existence, where we could function in total trust with all our fellow human beings, things would be different. If everyone exhibited only the highest standards of ethical behavior, benevolence, compassion, and empathy, we would not need boundaries.

Obviously, that is not where we are, and no one is suggesting that we shouldn't be prudent and avoid danger. But a closer look will illustrate what I am talking about.

As I have explained before, the word "yoga" comes from the Sanskrit root "yug" which means to "yoke, connect, unite." The union is between soul and spirit. If spirit permeates all of creation, what soul could be more connected to spirit than an unborn baby?

The soul of the baby, unbound by the confines of the physical body and immersed in the creation of the body, has the closest connection with creation possible. And we were all there during that process You and me and everyone else walking around in a body.

So, when I am talking about being immersed, I'm not talking about a casual connection or a "meaningful encounter." I'm talking about being completely saturated, engrossed, submerged, and connected to the surrounding environment. The "connected" state of yoga.

We come into this world very comfortable in our immersed state of mind. You can perceive it in the little child. As they exist in their helpless state, they are neutral and passive in what they see. That is, of course, until something makes them physically uncomfortable.

But that is a physical sensation and not a perception or attitude toward what they see.

They sustain this state of mind for quite some time. They move through the day connected to the experience of the moment and move on to the experience of the next moment. They aren't distracted by things in the past. They aren't worried about future events.

And, like it or not, that is the healthiest way to go through life. Take care of the moment, and don't be affected by *non-productive, damaging, mental activity of worrying and being distracted by past events or unknown future possibilities.*

This is what the yogis mean by being "childlike." I've always reminded my daughter to "remember what it felt like to be a little kid." So, lately, I've been trying to heed my own advice.

In Eastern spiritual practices, meditation is usually the road to finding this state of mind. Meditation is beneficial on so many levels, and lately, I've used it to try to get back to that childlike state of mind.

As I sit, I try to take myself back to a scene I can remember as a little kid. The younger, the better. Then I try to tune into the state of mind that I had at that moment. It can be done. It is all there in your memory.

Once I connect to that feeling I just want to experience that frame of mind. From there it is like "muscle memory." The goal, for me, is to get so familiar with that feeling that I can conjure it when I need it, like during times of stress, hurt or frustration.

We are so programmed in our culture to look for remedies outside of ourselves, usually in a paid for consumable product. Whether it be therapy, exercise, pills, drugs, food, etc., it is really all the same. We seek relief for our suffering from "something." Of course, this approach rarely gives lasting comfort, since it usually only relieves symptoms or offers intellectual answers to an emotional issue.

So, if you are into it, give it a try. Also, when you are around little kids, try to tune in to their vibe. I know to some people this will sound like a load of crap, and that is fine. I'm not going to argue for fine and subtle points in the context of a coarse and crude reality.

But here is the deal. *The more you discredit, disbelieve, and devalue the true abilities and power you possess to manage your life, the more you limit those abilities.* A trinity of "D's!" Remember, affirming and acknowledging limitations only makes them more real for you.

We were never meant to be launched into this game without the tools to self-maintain and repair ourselves. We were not meant to have to "buy" a service or products to heal us or make us complete. We are all just sold on the self-limiting, collective consciousness into which we have been born, bred, and bamboozled.

OK, a trinity of "B's." That is the third trinity of words in a sentence in this chapter with the same first letter! A trinity of trinities! I'm gonna quit while I'm ahead.

Chapter 20

The Yoga of Karma

> *"Do unto others as you would have them do unto you." - Luke 6:31*

Karma Yoga, or the "yoga of action" is one of the more fascinating, and probably one of the more misunderstood, aspects of yoga.

In the West, people tend to associate karma with such ideas as "If I do good things, good things will happen to me; If I do bad things, bad things will happen to me; what goes around, comes around," etc.

People love to embrace the idea of karma when the good things are happening to them. However, when bad things are happening to them, they tend to wonder how things can be so "unfair."

This flawed reasoning also shows up in their view of others as well. When someone they like is succeeding, they say, "Oh that's so great; she is amazing. She deserves it."

But when someone they hate has great luck or fortune, it is a different story. Then it's, "How can that horrific scumbag get all that?" Uh, maybe he did something to deserve it? Something we don't know anything about?

On a side note, this is a classic example of how this physical existence is nothing but constantly changing scenery. It is only our perception of it that gives us our feelings.

Newton's Law

We will look at a commonly sighted law of the physical universe that is sometimes associated with karma. That is Newton's third law. "For every action, there is an equal and opposite reaction."

This is a simple way to for people to sum up karma so they can move on to the important stuff, like handstands and celebrity gossip. It, unfortunately, does not have anything to do with karma.

Newton's application was to physics, and to two physical objects reacting in contact with each other. A simple example of this would be when you sit in a chair. Your body exerts a downward force on the chair, and the chair exerts an upward force on your body. The direction of the force of the first object is *opposite* to the force of the second object. This is an example of "action-reaction force pairs."

So, if I were to shoot someone, while Newton's law would apply to the bullet and the object it strikes, it would have no application to the consequences of my action.

My reason for giving this little lesson in physics is to educate, entertain and illustrate that it is not related to karma. The physical plane is not the spiritual plane, and the same laws do not necessarily apply.

Karma Yoga

Karma and karma yoga are not the same thing, just as Bhakti or devotion is not the same as Bhakti Yoga. Both can exist without an application to yoga. But both can be used as a means to "yoga" or the connection we have already discussed.

To begin with let's look at the meaning of the Sanskrit word "karma." The straight translation is "action." Nothing more and nothing less. Obviously, with such a non-specific definition, it is open to all kinds of spins and interpretation.

Before we go deeper, there is something we must consider. There are two separate connections to our "actions" that affect karma in different ways. One is our *relationship to our actions,* and how that affects us internally. The other is the external *repercussions of our actions.*

First, we will deal with our relationship to our actions.

Two common and popular definitions of Karma Yoga are:

- "Selfless service."
- "Selfless action, as a way to perfection."

The problem with these definitions is in our understanding of the words "service" and "action."

To most people "service" implies an action directed toward benefitting something specific, usually a person or a cause.

Action, on the other hand, could be something as inconsequential to benefitting others as playing a musical instrument by yourself or meditating.

This is where things can get confusing. If we take the approach of "doing good things" then it would seem we would need a receiver of the activities, and that would be a service. If the approach is action, no recipient is necessary.

Since "karma" translates as action, and "action" encompasses a random activity as well as "service," we will choose action as a foundation.

Another key to this is the word that is used in both definitions...*selfless*.

The definition of "selfless" can be taken in different ways, but I will put it into terms I believe are in line with the yogic meaning.

Krishna's discourse in *The Bhagavad Gita* is considered by many to be the primary source of information regarding Karma Yoga. And like so many other ancient texts, it can be interpreted in many ways.

Be that as it may, the term "selfless," as implied by Krishna in the Gita, and by my definition would be: *"without attachment to personal outcome."*

And there is that most important word once again...*Attachment*.

As I have mentioned before and will mention again, in yoga and Buddhism, attachment is considered the primary source of human suffering. And remember, *negative attachment (anger, hatred, fear, etc.) and positive attachment are both just as possessive and spiritually limiting.*

Regardless of the version of the Gita you read, Krishna is very clear about this. He emphasizes, more than once; *"non-attachment to the fruits (results) of your actions."*

From this perspective, "service" to others is not an issue. *Whether the action involves service or not, the importance is in the non-attachment.*

This practice can free us, not only from attachment problems of the present but also from past attachments and potential future attachments.

Non-attachment is not non-caring or apathy in the performance of our actions. In fact, Krishna holds us to a very high standard for the quality of the things we do. The non-attachment is meant to manage the severity of our emotional responses to possible outcomes of the action.

This is in line with Buddha's teaching of attachment being the source of suffering. By removing our expectation and attachment to results, we minimize potential suffering.

But the quality of the action is never compromised.

Krishna tells us we are to do our best, in all we do, because we have a role in this incarnation.

We should perform our role, the very best we can with no attachment to glory or reward, for the sake of honoring the creator and director of this creation...Spirit.

We meditate and pray, and through "yoga," attune ourselves to our true path, our dharma. Then we offer our work to Spirit. The name we give the creator/ director, whose vision we serve in this play of life, does not matter.

So, in a sense, this is a practice of non-attached service - service to Spirit and creation.

By doing this with an open heart and no ego attachment, we are freed from the mental turmoil caused by the results, either achieved or denied, of our actions and expectations.

How and why we are cast in the roles we play is not based on a clean slate. Past attachments and karma (both positive and negative) are manifesting in the present until we work through them.

Thus, the combined effects of what we would call "our karma."

I want to close this part by saying that there are other technical reasons for the creation and perpetuation of the things that follow us around and affect our lives and our happiness. This is the subject of "samskaras" and "the Gunas," etc.

That subject is too much to get into here and is not relevant to this book. It is not necessary to understand the mechanics of an internal combustion engine to have a car take you places. Yoga methods only need to be practiced. It only matters that the methods take you where you want to go.

Suffice it to say, according to yoga, if you follow Krishna's advice all will be well.

"As You Sow, So Shall You Reap"

Now we will explore how most people relate to karma, the idea of "if I do good things, I get good things, and if I do bad things, I get bad things."

As far as a reason for good behavior, let's just accept something for the moment.

Most major religions and spiritual practices in this world have a recommended code of behavior. Some examples would be the Ten Commandments, the Eight Precepts of Buddhism, and the Yamas and Niyamas of Hinduism.

To make this easy let's assume, for the moment, that the creators of these codes knew that good behavior was necessary for a happy spiritual experience.

The obvious problem here is, what constitutes good and bad action or behavior? If I kill someone who is killing other people, and I save lives, does that change the fact that I killed him?

Or, if I witness injustice or harm that I could stop, but I choose not to act, to "not get involved," is my inaction condoning and aiding the crime? Is my choice to not act a cause for "bad karma?" This is not a simple question. For me, there is a formula I use.

In one of the Star Trek movies, Spock sacrifices himself to save the lives of the entire ship. He doesn't want to die, and Kirk doesn't want him to die, but he tells Kirk, "The needs of the many outweigh the needs of the few."

That is a pretty fair measure of any action. Does the action do the greatest good for the greatest number? And that "number" is not limited to humans - are there other life forms involved? The environment, the group, the culture?

Generally speaking, the idea of karma in this sense, "As you sow, so shall you reap," is attributed to "cause and effect." It should be noted that the idea of cause and effect is not a scientific law like Newton's third law. It is more a philosophical concept, and many will argue that there is no hard science to support it.

So what about the good behavior? What about "cause and effect"? For the answer to that, we must go back to the start of all this.

Do unto others as you would have them do unto you. Luke 6:31

It has been my experience, that very little is left to chance when it comes to spiritual scriptures. The Bible is no exception.

Of all the great sayings, parables, stories and lessons in the Bible, the above line has been singled out as the "Golden rule."

I am sure the trolls would be happy to jump on that statement and say, "Yeah, well what if I am into pain, or being spit on, then I can do it to others, right?" To that, I say; The levels of insanity and aberration on this planet are quite appalling." Some people are just not very evolved spiritually, and to argue or debate with them is a waste of time.

So we are going to assume, for the sake of discussion among those at the higher end of the spiritual food chain, that the Golden Rule is a reasonable request.

We can look at "cause and effect" in terms of the obvious. If I cut someone with a knife and wound them, the knife is the cause, and the wound is the effect. But how does that action come back to me?

At this point, I am going to bring something into this discussion that I do not, typically, see addressed in opinions and theories on karma and good behavior. Although it may appear that I am going off course, the point of what I am about to say comes back to answer the above question.

There is a fundamental tenet of yoga, as well as in many other spiritual traditions. That is at the core of it all when every single extraneous thing has been stripped away, that we are all one. To put it bluntly, when we remove the ego, the personality, the attachments and the neurosis, the identity, the personality, the physical, astral, causal bodies, and every single other thing aside from spirit, *I am you, and you are me.*

We have lived in a confined individual identity for so long that the true reality of being one with others is impossible for us to grasp.

The wording of the Golden Rule implies this. The lack of separation means there is no difference between what is good or bad for you or me and what is good or bad for someone else.

We all know that when we do beneficial things to and for ourselves, mentally, physically or spiritually, we experience the rewards. By the same token when we do things that are damaging or unhealthy we experience the downside as well.

Since we are one with everything, anything we do, either beneficial or damaging to others, we are simultaneously doing to ourselves. As such, we will experience the results of those actions.

What this means is that when I stab someone with a knife, I am at the same time stabbing myself., and I will ultimately suffer the consequences of that. Naturally, I don't experience the physical pain at that moment, but the intention and execution of the action create the karmic effect.

Those consequences may not happen right away, or even soon. But this is a very long and very deep path we travel.

Remember that thing you are experiencing that seems so unfair? Well...

But it is not only our personal actions that have repercussions. There is collective karma as well. The behavior of groups toward other groups, other life forms, the planet, the environment, all generate consequence. It all comes into play.

Here is the good news.

The potential effects of past actions are not being thrown at us all at once. In yoga, these potential effects are referred to as "seeds" of karma. They are like seeds waiting to sprout when environmental circumstances activate them.

Again, for the sake of this discussion, it is not necessary to understand the mechanics of this. What is important to understand is that yoga has given us a way not to have to work through all those seeds.

By using various yoga techniques (meditation, pranayama, bhakti, etc.,) it is possible to "burn the seeds of past karma" before they sprout. The result of this is a "hastening" or speeding up of forward spiritual progress.

Speeding spiritual evolution is the ultimate outcome of applying the science of yoga. It is considered that we will all eventually arrive at the same place. It is a question of how much suffering and drama we choose to endure, and for how long.

Yoga is NOT gymnastics. It is not social media "likes." This is a journey so deep, and far beyond asana and the "yoga" we see today, as to be unrecognizable.

It is a journey that few undertake, with a destination at which few arrive. But no effort is wasted, and there is great value in the journey itself. The challenge is to begin and maintain the practice. To use the famous quote by Lao Tzu, *"The journey of a thousand miles begins with a single step."*

Chapter 21

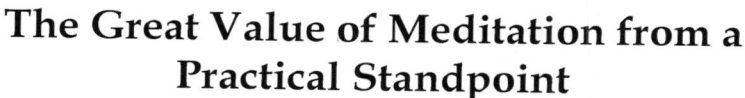

The Great Value of Meditation from a Practical Standpoint

> *"Spiritual advancement is not to be displayed by one's outward powers, but solely by the depth of his bliss in meditation."* - *Paramahansa Yogananda*

I find it rather amusing that after thousands of years of Eastern spiritual practitioners advocating the benefits of meditation, there has now been a big "discovery" by science that it is, in fact, a good thing. Thank goodness, the guys in white lab coats have machines that measure brain activity and have given us the "OK," so we can feel comfortable sitting and being quiet.

Spiritual practitioners, advocating meditation, assume that we would have enough *intuitive* ability to recognize something as valuable as meditation, but some folks need their science!

The irony of it is that meditation helps give us access to the intuition that we needed in the first place to know it was a good thing! Ah well, life is like that.

So, what is the value of meditation? Pretty simple: To help us function better mentally, feel better emotionally and spiritually, and possibly be healthier physically. It is not, in itself, an outcome. It is an *enhancement to attaining the outcome.*

Different schools of meditation take different approaches and directions toward their specific desired outcomes. For the sake of this piece, I will just deal with how meditation affects mental activity and how that improves things.

It has been promoted for a very long time by yoga, and now by quantum physics that our "consciousness" affects the reality we experience. This is the subject of entire books so I won't get into the mechanics of it.

But assuming this is the case, then obviously the quality and clarity of that consciousness is going to be a significant factor, and influence, on our reality. *Meditation is the science by which we can bring clarity and focus to that consciousness.*

First, we must consider that we are not our thoughts. We are the "viewer" and user of the thoughts. The viewer is pure consciousness, and not the thought or emotion arising from it.

We, the viewers, sift through the thoughts that arise from our perception of the things going on around us, or even thoughts that randomly occur.

Some we notice, some we don't, some we search for to accomplish specific tasks. And some of the thoughts create an emotional response in us. None of this is the viewer, but the viewer is affected by all of this. Often the viewer becomes lost in this process, and sometimes this becomes counterproductive to our existence. We become reactive or negatively triggered by the process, and lose our objectivity and happiness. This is where meditation comes in.

This ongoing mental activity results in a mental "restlessness" in our perception, that can be compared to static or interference in a radio channel. *Meditation is a process of "clearing the static" of restless mental processes that diminish the clarity of our perception.* By quieting the restlessness and agitation of the mind, we can use that clarity to our benefit.

We can use that clarity to improve learning new information, channeling artistic inspiration, or acquiring spiritual perspective.

As for physical benefits, meditation is great for managing stress. Stress is, in my opinion, the most significant contributor to chronic disease. Meditation can reduce stress and anxiety and benefit health.

Meditation is not an easy habit to develop or maintain. It seems hard and boring and not a source of the instant gratification to which we have become accustomed. That is our fault and that of our ego, not the meditation.

It has been proven in many studies that meditation changes brain chemistry in ways that take us out of our ego, or "I-ness," identity, and increases our ability to experience our connection with all things. In that spiritual state, we can experience the truth of our situation. *We clear the connection to that place through meditation.*

If your interest is in acquiring knowledge, learning will be more efficient with the clarity and focus acquired in meditation. If you are a person of devotion, your connection and love will manifest in meditation. If you are a person of faith, your belief will deepen and so on.

It seems that people become interested in the benefits of a practice like meditation when they are under duress and feel the need of some help, but there is a problem with this. Without the familiarity and habit of meditation, the efforts are as a beginner.

Developing a good meditation practice is an acquired skill, and takes a little time. We need to develop that skill when we are feeling good. Then, when hard times come, we are ready and prepared. This is not an easy sell. When everything is going well, how many people save money for when the recession hits? Not many.

If you are happy and content with all aspects of your life, none of this seems to matter. However, since nothing is certain in life, except change, now is a good time to start your meditation practice. Find a meditation technique that resonates with you, put it to practice, and get good at it. It just might prove to be the "lifeboat" you need down the road.

Part Three
Cancer

Chapter 22

Cancer

The Worthy Opponent

> *"If you know the enemy and know yourself, you need not fear the result of a hundred battles. If you know yourself but not the enemy, for every victory gained you will also suffer a defeat. If you know neither the enemy nor yourself, you will succumb in every battle."*
> *-Sun Tzu, The Art of War*

Life is the arena in which our battles are waged. Yoga is the armory of weapons we will use. The opponents are many.

For our purposes, I have chosen cancer as the worthy opponent. There are many from which to choose: depression, addiction, physical injury, unhappy relationships, among many others I have chosen cancer for three reasons.

- It is definitely a "worthy' opponent.

- I have first-hand experience with it.
- I want to use this opportunity to inform people.

It is essential to know the enemy.

Be it cancer or any other opponent on the battlefield of life, the prerequisite to success in battle is knowing everything you can about the enemy. Research, education, and inquiry into whatever you are dealing with must be done.

While the principles are the same for all the problems/enemies we face, I will speak about cancer. It is perhaps the most misunderstood, and for all the wrong reasons, of the tragic enemies we face.

This presentation on cancer serves as an example of research into "knowing your enemy." In the process, it also gives some short, concise and essential information to the average person regarding some truths about cancer.

If you are not interested in this, you can skip ahead to the next section of the book. That being said, I think knowledge about cancer, in these times, is extremely valuable.

Chapter 23

Cancer Introduction

Knowing the enemy.

There are many problems that, when they arise, allow you time to research and make plans for dealing with them. For example, if you realize you have an addiction problem, hopefully, you will have time to learn about potential causes, treatments, support, etc.

If you want to lose weight, you probably won't die or be forced into a program with severe side effects without time to do research. Same applies to divorce, financial problems and most other situations.

As I will explain here, cancer is not like that. You often will not have the luxury of time or state of mind, to understand and "know' your enemy.

Sometimes you need that spare tire.

Let me ask you something. Do you have a first-aid kit? Do you have a spare tire?

Hopefully, you answered yes. Not because you know you will need them, but because you *may* need them.

You have them "just in case."

It is precisely the same thing with information. It is important to know what to do in the event of a power outage, an earthquake, a gas leak, or even a zombie apocalypse.

These may not be life or death situations (well, maybe the zombies), but knowledge could make the experience more pleasant, safer or at least less stressful.

It is "just in case" emergency information. However, there is a problem with cancer. No one seems to have, or feel the need for life-saving "emergency information."

They may think "It's too unpleasant, too boring or too scary. Or they think, "It'll never happen to me. If it does, I'll deal with it then." This is flawed thinking.

If you were a man, and I told you that you had a 1 in 2 chance of getting into an unpleasant situation, and a 1 in 4 chance of dying from that situation you would, of course, want the "emergency information," right?

If you were a woman, and I told you that you had a 1 in 3 chance of getting into an unpleasant situation, and a 1 in 5 chance of dying from it, you'd also want that "emergency Information" right?

These odds are from The American Cancer Society.

Of all the things that you do not want to be ill-prepared for, a cancer diagnosis should be very high on that list.

Here is the reason that knowledge is so valuable. If you get that diagnosis, and you don't have the "emergency information," it will be too late.

You will be overwhelmed and paralyzed with fear, a "deer in the headlights."

You will be told, "You must act NOW! Chemo, radiation, surgery! We can't let it spread! We must deal with it now!

And you will look hopefully at the doctor, and say, "Yes, yes, just take care of it."

And in that state, you will be ramrodded through the AMA / FDA / Big Pharma/ Insurance machine: a one size fits all cash cow.

I am not condoning or condemning it. It is the treatment model. And unfortunately, as cancer statistics show, this is not a great model.

People will say, "Yes, but what good will knowledge do? It will get treated the only way it can be treated." Thinking that is the biggest mistake of all.

Choices need to be informed.

Even within the parameters of standard medicine, there are options and choices. For instance:

- What method of radiation, and who will do it? Why is their way better?
- What protocol and what specific chemo is available. What are the different risks, effectiveness, or side effects of the different ones?
- What are the least invasive and lowest risk to reward surgery options?

Of course, there are many other choices and decisions to be made along the way. And you know what? Just like any other merchant, the doctor you see will sell you only the goods he carries. It is what he knows, what he "has in stock," and the brand he uses.(This also applies to alternative/integrative supplemental doctors and clinics as well.)

Just like a washing machine, his brand might be very good, but not necessarily be the one best suited to your needs.

Since I started writing about cancer, I have had people come to me and say something like this. "My (fill in the blank relation) has (fill in the blank cancer), and was told he/she needs to do (fill in the blank protocol), and is terrified and depressed and doesn't know what to do. What do you think?"

I must make something very, very clear here and now. I will never give medical advice or recommendations. I would never assume the responsibility or liability. I only provide *information* based on my *personal experience*, and *most importantly, based on my opinions*.

I say "What have they done? What are the options? Who have they seen?"

They may reply along the line of something like "Well, they had surgery or radiation, and now the doctor wants them to do chemo, more radiation, or hormone therapy," or whatever.

I am sorry, and I don't want to sound like I lack compassion, but it is very late for this conversation. There are still plenty of things they can do, but they should have been armed with all the "emergency information" the day they were diagnosed.

So that is what this part of the book is all about. If someone who has cancer and reads this, and get something from it, I am beyond happy.

If you are dealing with someone who has cancer, perhaps this will help you understand the world of cancer.

But, most importantly, if you don't have cancer and you read it, and are diagnosed, here is my hope;

That the day you step onto to that battlefield, for what may well be the greatest fight of your life, that you are armed with every bit of tactical knowledge and weapon available to you.

Chapter 24

Cancer and Me...How I Roll

> "Ultimately life is disease, death, and oblivion.
> It's still better than high school." - Dan Savage

I am not going to tell the story of my diagnosis at this time. After being diagnosed, my traditional medical choices were surgery or radiation. At that point, I was given some excellent advice.

The doctor told me that my cancer was slow growing, and to take a little time to research the doctors and techniques available. I don't think that he had in mind where that would lead me.

I need to make something perfectly clear that is a prerequisite to understanding how I ended up where I did, and why this approach is not for everyone.

I am a yogi. I don't mean I "do" yoga. What follows, you will either understand or not, and that is ok.

I have discussed at length attachment and the view of yoga and Buddhism on the pitfalls surrounding it. That understanding of attachment must extend to this life. For me, it is easier because I have led an incredibly full, and relatively long life. I am fully aware that to deal with this type of disease at a younger age would be quite different.

That said, there were a couple of times when I was quite young that the possibility of death was very real. By that, I am not talking about something like, "Wow man, I wiped out on a huge, wave and thought I was gonna drown." I mean for real. And even in those moments, I remember thinking, "Well if this is it, I just kinda wish I'd had time to do more things."

So, maybe to some degree, an acceptance of life and death came naturally to me. But yoga has only helped reinforce it. An awareness of the possibilities beyond the body goes a long way. The mental and spiritual insights that yoga can provide are beyond measure.

I am not afraid of death. My spiritual practice has been in place for a long time. I don't look forward to the dying part, but I think the death part may be very nice. This matters because I am committed to not sacrificing quality of life only to linger in a compromised physical condition in this world.

However, that does not mean that I would not try to overcome a health challenge. The value of lessons learned, and possibilities gained from the problems life deals us, are the reason we play this game. Had I not fought the opponent, I would not have learned the things I have, and you wouldn't be reading this.

As I made the rounds to specialists and hospitals, it was apparent that the traditional treatments all had a very high probability of long-term side effects that I was not willing to accept. This is one of the main problems with cancer. Fear of the treatments and side effects is often as bad as the fear of the disease itself. And that fear is often manipulated by doctors and alternative practitioners.

One doctor, at a well-advertised hospital cancer center, tried for the fear tactic. During our interview, when it came up that I had been scheduled to have rotator cuff (shoulder) surgery, he informed me that my whole body would feel like my torn shoulder when the cancer metastasized to my bones.

Now, there's a genuine compassionate healer for you.

After a while, it became clear to me that I would at least try alternative protocols before risking the side effects of the "standard treatment." I soon discovered something that I hadn't expected.

As I embarked on my journey of clinics and online support groups, I did not meet one other person for whom alternative therapy was his or her first choice. Everyone else had either tried all the standard medical treatments without success and was very bad off, or were doing alternative as a supplemental treatment to chemo or radiation.

I did the various diets-vegan, vegetarian, ketogenic, paleo, macrobiotic. I did the cleanses and parasite treatments. I took the supplements, at one point 58 pills a day. I sat in lazy boy recliners with an IV in my arm for hours. I had my blood sent to Greece. I did Rife, UVB, colonics, lymph drainage, Budwig. I did the cancer cascade.

I spent a lot of money. I saw people come and go, and I mean literally go. All the time this was going on, and for several years, I was reading and researching everything I could find regarding therapies, clinical trials, studies, and breakthroughs.

I've read books and watched films on physical, mental and spiritual healing. I've searched the Internet, subscribed to health and medical newsletters. I now know way more about cancer and different therapies and protocols than I ever wanted to know.

The reason I am even writing this is that I feel the information is important. It is also primarily experiential, and that is not common. As I roll along through this information, see it for what it is: mostly first-hand knowledge and opinion being passed along from a journey on a path less traveled.

Chapter 25

Are You in Remission?

Of the many things that come up in cancer conversations, this is one of the hardest for me to wrap my head around. Let's break it down.

Are you in remission? From a yoga standpoint, "I" am pure spirit occupying a physical body of which I am not. I am timeless, ageless and indestructible, so there is nothing for me to be in remission from.

Next, we figure the body is not in remission. So, that leaves us with, "Is the cancer in remission?" This is not easily answered.

The not very pleasant fact is that cancer, viruses, bacteria, germs, and whatnot are present in and around us all the time. Our bodies are a constant battlefield waging war between our immune systems and the invaders. When everything is working right, the immune system is winning.

We all have abnormal cells in our systems, at all times. Our amazing bodies deal with that.

However, if they don't deal with it 100%, we don't know it until symptoms manifest.

Most cancers take a long time to develop to the point of even becoming tumors. Years, in fact. During that time, while you were feeling good and running 10ks and having children, you, in fact, were not in remission. You were just at a level where you were not affected.

So if you ask me, "Are you in remission?" I honestly would say, "I don't know. I feel good, and people tell me I look good and I'm not losing weight. I haven't had tests in a while, so I don't know about that, so what say we just get along with what we were doing 'cuz if I sit here and focus on cancer, I'm just gonna attract it to me more." (as per the law of attraction)

So, the question is whether the cancer is getting bigger, smaller or staying the same, and is it affecting your life? Generally, if the "numbers" are "better," you are doing good. If not, well...but the numbers can fluctuate. Any improvement or decline is rarely ever a straight trajectory either up or down.

If the cancer is staying the same and not affecting you, then what is the difference? If you have a 30-year stalemate with cancer and die of a heart attack, did it make any difference? This is what some cancer survivors who may have an inoperable tumor, that never grows or goes away, call "living with cancer."

And by the way, is that any different from your body continually fighting off smaller amounts of cancer every day? As yoga teaches us, with all things in life, attachment causes suffering. Attachment to numbers is no exception. People who are diagnosed with cancer, and who live and breathe by numbers can have a tough time, and the stress of the obsession can cause more harm than good.

So, you can see the complexity of all this, and this doesn't even involve the multitude of reasons, physical or mental, for getting sick in the first place, or the protocols to remedy the disease.

Perhaps a better inquiry than, "Are you in remission?" would be, "how are you doing?" or "How are you feeling?" or if you must, "How are your numbers?"

Because the person diagnosed with cancer could ask you all the very same questions... Even, "Are you in remission?"

Chapter 26

How I Got Cancer

This is where I will start...with a story

A Day in the Life

The alarm goes off at 4:30 a.m. I fumble to turn it off as I become aware of the sinking feeling in my gut as my brain begins to register where I am and what I need to do.

It's Monday and my call time at work is 5:42 a.m. It is a normal call time for a Monday on the set of a TV show or movie. Sometimes it is earlier, but rarely ever later, on a Monday.

Of course, as the week progresses the calls will get later and later until Friday. Then it could be noon, 1 o'clock or even later. Or maybe 4 or 5 pm for the dreaded "night shoot."

I brush my teeth and get dressed. I showered the night before so that I could sleep as late as possible. I gather any reading material I might want for the day and head out the door.

I get a cup of coffee on the way and drink it. The thought of the week ahead and the potential stress and drama makes me sad and anxious.

I walk into the hair and makeup trailer, and already there is an oppressive energy in the air. One of the actresses is in the hair chair. She is puffy eyed and telling everyone about the big fight she had the night before with her totally inappropriate boyfriend.

Of course, everyone is fawning over her with sympathy and commiseration. This is evidently an earth-shattering event, even though it occurs every week or two.

I have learned that the addiction to drama is very real. Maybe there should be a twelve-step program for drama addiction: Dramaholics Anonymous, International Headquarters, Hollywood, California, USA.

Two actors come in. One sits in my chair, and the other goes to makeup. They have had good weekends, and are ready to hold court and one-up each other with clever and witty banter and comebacks.

I enjoy this. It's entertaining and brings some levity to the downer that was happening earlier.

The distressed actress huddles into quiet anxiety with her makeup artist, no longer the center of attention.

Next comes one of my actresses to my chair. She is generally fine, but today the weather is foggy and humid. Humid means we fight frizzy hair.

As we work through it the process, I can see the shift. She begins to narrow her focus on her hair, and it is like a switch flips. We go into the obsessive mode.

Finally, after draining as much of my energy as she can, she is happy. The bummer is that the result would have been the same if she'd sat there, on her phone, and texted and tweeted or whatever, and it would have taken less time.

Now there is a new problem. An actress was late getting here and had a wardrobe fitting that took too long as well. Now she is running late for getting through "the works." She is in makeup and late to the set.

The person in charge of making sure actors get to where they need to be on time is not happy. He has a headset, and his superior is in his ear demanding time estimates every two minutes. He is afraid to ask makeup for another estimate because the last time he did she snapped back,

"The more you keep asking me, the longer it takes!"

Finally, the late actress is done and off to set. In walks the next higher up person in charge. I am avoiding titles because it wouldn't mean anything unless you were in the business. "What the hell happened?" he demands. Then the back-peddling and blame game begins.

It seems to be a rule in Hollywood to never, ever, under any circumstance, take the blame for anything - even if it involves throwing everyone involved, including your mother if necessary, under the bus.

I did her hair but managed to get it done in much less than my "allotted time" so, thank God, I'm in the clear on this one, and my mother is safe.

Then we go off to set, and it is business as usual. Wardrobe fixes the lay of collars, buttons, and necklaces and smooths wrinkles. Makeup is on the shine and lips. I chase flyaway hairs and sagging curls.

While the camera roles, we are buried in phones, tablets, and the occasional magazine. A few actors come in throughout the day, and we get them ready.

As our tired and sleep-deprived bodies begin to fade and crave energy, we are drawn to the craft service table. This is a place of food and beverage, available all day, that is populated almost exclusively with processed carbohydrates, non-organic foods, sugary treats, sodas, and coffee.

All things designed to provide fast energy and motivation to a body that, in fact, needs sleep and rest.

Other than that, we will sit on set. We have a half hour catered lunch that will consist of food prepared from the most cost-effective (cheapest) ingredients available. If we are lucky, we will wrap by 7:30 pm.

Since general crew call was 7 am, and with a half hour for lunch, this is a 12-hour day for the crew, which is considered optimal by the Accounting Department. However, it is not uncommon to work much longer hours.

My personal record is 23.5 hours, and 15 hours is not at all unusual. Since our department always comes in before the crew, today I have been at work for nearly fourteen hours.

I will make the 40-minute drive (without traffic) home. I will take a shower, go to bed and start the same routine tomorrow.

And I will do it day after day, week after week, month after month, for ten months of the year, year after year.

Some people think my job is glamorous.

Chapter 27

Why I Got Cancer

In the previous chapter, I described a typical workday during my time in film and television production.

I want to make it clear that I am not complaining about my life. I am grateful to have been employed and to have been able to provide material needs for my family and myself.

The obvious health hazards of the type of work I described are as follows;

- Stress
- Poor sleep
- Bad diet
- Lack of exercise

Stress.

Stress is the number one destroyer of health. Period. The hormonal imbalances created in the *unnaturally extended* states of stress-induced fight or flight biochemistry, to which we are subjected in modern society, are something the human body was never meant to endure.

These hormonal imbalances directly, and negatively, affect the immune system, and thus our body's ability to fight off or control chronic disease.

Every single cancer survivor or patient that I have had the conversation with, regarding their illness, has told me they *can trace the origin back to a time of severe stress or trauma.* Make no mistake. **That is every single one.**

Sleep

"Sleep is that golden chain that ties health and our bodies together."- Thomas Dekker

Irregular, inconsistent and insufficient sleep is next, although diet is, no doubt, comparable. I have, however, put sleep next to stress, because it is a hormone problem as well.

I do not want to get too technical or carried away here, but it is impossible to overestimate the complexity and essential functions of circadian rhythms in virtually all living things, from the most complex animals to plants and microbes.

Here are a couple of quotes from a 2011 research paper titled "Genetics of Circadian Rhythms in Mammalian Model Organisms."

"Circadian rhythms are physical, mental and behavioral changes that follow a roughly 24-hour cycle, responding primarily to light and darkness in an organism's environment. They are found in most living things, including animals, plants and many tiny microbes. The study of circadian rhythms is called chronobiology."

"The rising and setting of the sun each day causes predictable environmental changes to which most organisms on earth have adapted by evolving endogenous biological timing systems with a period of approximately 24 hours. These circadian (~24 hr.) clocks anticipate environmental cycles and control daily rhythms in biochemistry, physiology, and behavior."

Take note of that last sentence. You cannot get much more inclusive as to the absolute imperative aspects of any living creature than, "...*biochemistry, physiology and behavior.*"

What this means is that we are programmed to live in "rhythm" cycles of waking and sleeping. The body relies on those cycles to produce the appropriate hormones for the functions of that cycle. During sleep, beneficial hormones for health and repair are released. During waking hours, hormones to increase focus, energy alertness, etc. are released.

When the waking and sleeping patterns are continually being changed, the body does not have time to readjust the hormonal release. It is trying to find the "rhythm." When hormones are unbalanced, the immune system suffers.

Between hormone imbalance from stress and a constantly disrupted circadian rhythm, the immune system can become severely compromised.

Diet.

"No disease that can be treated by diet should be treated with any other means." - Maimonides

Diet is the most widely accepted contributor to health. It is not hard to see why. The food and beverages we consume have the most obvious measurable responses.

Eat something bad, throw up. Drink too much, get a hangover. Too much caffeine, get the jitters. Too much food over time, we gain weight. Not enough food over time, we lose weight.

Getting people to agree that diet affects health is not the problem. But getting them to do something about it, evidently, is.

Frankly, I don't even know where to begin with that, and I won't try. I will get into some of the how and why of food and disease, but I have no idea what has created the psychosis and neurosis surrounding food.

The degree to which people are willing to sacrifice their health, happiness, appearance, physical capabilities, opportunities and overall quality of life for the sake of eating something is beyond my grasp. I'm sure that has been the focus of thousands of studies and many books and papers.

This quote from a 2011 published paper titled "The western diet and lifestyle and diseases of civilization" sums the basic idea up quite nicely.

"This mismatch between our ancient physiology and the western diet and lifestyle underlies many so-called diseases of civilization, including coronary heart disease, obesity, hypertension, type 2 diabetes, epithelial cell cancers, autoimmune disease, and osteoporosis, which are rare or virtually absent in hunter-gatherers and other non-westernized populations. It is therefore proposed that the adoption of diet and lifestyle that mimic the beneficial characteristics of the PR agricultural environment is an effective strategy to reduce the risk of chronic degenerative diseases."

Here, again, I think the discipline of a physical and spiritual yoga practice, can be of great help. Most serious yoga practitioners, I know, don't seem to have problems with unhealthy food obsessions, excess, and control.

Exercise.

There is nothing about the thousands of generations of genetic adaptation that came before now that, in any way, has prepared our bodies, in any way, for a life of sitting for 8-12 hours a day. Combine time at a desk, time in a car, time in front of the computer or TV, time at the dinner table or at a bar, or hopefully, time meditating, and you could easily rack up 12 hours.

That may be unavoidable. What is available to counteract the horrific effects of this completely unnatural lifestyle is exercise.

Again, not a mystery to anyone.

And yet, something with such proven and tangible rewards as energy, vitality, appearance, and health in general, is such a battle of will for so many.

Many people attack exercise from the wrong perspective. They set unreasonable goals or start at too high a level of difficulty. They then become overwhelmed, discouraged and give up.

If you want to succeed with exercise, you absolutely must choose something you enjoy doing, at a level you are comfortable with. It is far better to take a nice walk every day than to join a gym, and never go.

The many forms of physical yoga are an excellent choice for people in any condition. Yoga can be practiced at so many different levels and with such varied approaches, that everyone can find something that will benefit them. The hard part is sorting through all that is available. You have got to find highly experienced teachers and talk to people, in similar situations to your own regarding choices.

· I'm Not Alone

Naturally, my occupation in the film industry is not the only one with these potential health hazards.

Nurses, who work long shifts and flip back and forth between days and nights, law enforcement, firefighters, and other emergency responders, as well as people who travel a lot into different time zones. Anyone who works long irregular hours of any kind is susceptible to the effects of irregular sleep.

Since my occupation is union-based (not just hair and makeup, but all the crafts) and involves insurance, pensions, and benefits, the health and mortality statistics of the members are very accurate.

Although I have heard various statistics on the longevity of our members, all are extraordinarily bad and far below the average human lifespan.

Some of the trades fare better than others, but I consider the long-term statistics to be evidence of the unfortunate health effects of this kind of work schedule.

There are aspects of this lifestyle that we can control easily, and those that we cannot. The one that is perhaps most easily dealt with is diet. Exercise and stress require more time and discipline. Sleep is the most difficult to control in occupations that involve long hours, irregular shifts or varying times of day.

It is so important to understand the holistic, or as you could say, the "whole-istic" component of health.

We tend to isolate things and look for specific remedies for specific situations, but the truth is that it is all connected. As in all things the chain is only as strong as the weakest link. Improving one or two things will help, but many things work together to create a synchronistic strength.

If you work an eight or even nine-hour day during daylight hours, you have a considerable advantage in being able to create a healthy lifestyle for yourself. It still takes the desire, or need, and the discipline to make it happen.

I will be covering the different challenges of these points, and hopefully, provide some suggestions in the following chapters. Take an accurate and impartial look at your situation, and consider what you are doing well and what could improve.

Wherever you are, if you are above ground and breathing you have the power to build the best health possible, and can experience all the potential available to you!

Chapter 28

The ABC's of Cancer Part 1

DISCLAIMER: THIS DOCUMENT DOES NOT PROVIDE MEDICAL ADVICE

The information, including but not limited to, text, graphics, images and other material contained in this document are for informational purposes only. The purpose of this document is to promote broad consumer understanding and knowledge of various health topics. It is not intended to be a substitute for professional medical advice, diagnosis or treatment. Always seek the advice of your physician or other qualified healthcare provider with any questions you may have regarding a medical condition or treatment and before undertaking a new healthcare regimen, and never disregard professional medical advice or delay in seeking it because of something you have read in this document.

The Basics

All right then, it is time to get into the basics of cancer. This is information that everyone should be aware of. It is relevant to how people get it, why people get it and what it likes and needs to thrive.

This information is useful for anyone dealing with cancer and other chronic disease. It is also valuable, as well, for prevention. The information has been researched and in most cases scientifically proven. Where it is theoretical, or highly accepted but not scientifically proven, I will indicate that.

A Note.

I want to mention something here that is very important. In the past, what we were "allowed" to see and hear were much more easily controlled. I am not going all "conspiracy theory" here, but it is just an undeniable fact that any time fewer people control anything, the more power they possess to manipulate it.

This has been the case with media, since the beginning of time, until very recently. There are very powerful powers that be, that control hundreds of billions of dollars. They have no interest other than financially satisfying themselves and the people they serve. Historically, they have had a great deal of influence in all media.

It is only with the advent of the Internet, and especially social media, that smaller, less powerful voices have been given a platform to be heard. As much as I, and many others, struggle with social media and its disgusting downsides, it serves a valuable function in spreading information and revealing suppressed truth.

Much of the information now available regarding cancer and disease has been around and accepted for a long time in many parts of the world. It, however, was not easily accessed because it does not promote certain "profitable" enterprises. Enough said.

The Truths that Somehow Turn Out to be Untrue

The subject of cancer and many chronic diseases can appear complex and convoluted at times, but it isn't really. Part of the problem is that the medical field has made so many blanket statements with such authority over the years. The problem is that later when proven otherwise and they backpedal, the original misconception lingers on.

One example of this would be the assertion by the medical profession that the immune system has nothing to do with prevention or healing cancer. Doctors have commonly extolled this for many years. Yet, just the other day, I heard an ad on the radio for a major cancer hospital singing the praises of the "latest" in immunotherapy.

The use of immune boosting to fight disease has been common practice in many countries for many years.

Pressured by information becoming available to the masses, they have been forced to adapt. Naturally, their versions of improving the immune response involves outrageously expensive patented drugs.

Another is the "saturated fat" lie. Tufts University recently completed a meta-analysis involving 600,000 participants. Yes, that is right, Six hundred thousand.

They found no difference in mortality rate, from any cause, between butter eaters and non-butter eaters.

As much as I like a good "scientific analysis," this should have been obvious by another common but not often mentioned statistic. France, where probably more saturated fat is eaten than anywhere in the world, consistently has the lowest or second lowest rate of heart disease in the world. The U.S. is not even in the top 50 lowest rates of heart disease.

This is indicative of something that I find rather terrifying if it could possibly be true (wink, wink). Could it be collusion between FDA, AMA, big Pharma, and the big food corporations?

There is a lot more money in corn and canola oil than olive oil and butter.

Another example would be the assertion that cancer is caused by your genes, and if you have the gene, tough luck. Now the "new" idea is epigenetics. This is the belief that we have potential gene expressions that are modified or activated by variations that result from external or environmental factors that switch genes on and off.

I don't want to get more technical than that, or you and I might fall asleep. You can google it if you are interested. What it amounts to is that our genetic outcomes are not written in stone, and are influenced by different factors.

And yet, often when I get into cancer conversations with people, they say, "isn't it just in your genes? I mean if you got the gene, you're going to get it."

Cancer rates have risen drastically in the last 100 years. However, it doesn't take a whole lot of thought to figure out that after all these thousands of generations of humanity, the increase in cancer is not because our genes suddenly changed.

I have given three prominent examples here, but there are many others. The medical and pharmaceutical industries throw out their latest "truths" the way software companies throw out their beta versions and worry about fixing them later.

So, why do people get cancer and the biggest question, why are so many more people getting it? I will preface this by saying that although medicine in this country only now seems to be warming to this, in other countries and natural healing modalities, this has been commonly accepted for a long time:

In the majority (I did not say all) of cases of cancer and many chronic diseases, it is because of a compromised immune system.

The reason more and more people are getting cancer, and other chronic diseases is not because after all these years of evolution we are being born with weaker immune systems. It is because, since the 1950s and '60s, our environment and food systems have been more and more corrupted with elements that compromise our immune systems.

Our bodies are continuously dealing with invaders. Virus, bacteria, aberrant cells to name a few, along with repairing an injury. If you read the chapter titled "Are you in remission?" it deals with this subject.

The healthy body's ability to protect and repair itself is incredible. When it functions properly, it can deal with a vast majority of what we consider "chronic disease." It is such a tribute to the human body to see the abuse some people inflict on it, and yet they are still alive. Imagine the potential of a perfect immune system in a healthy body!

We don't need a degree in anything to understand a fundamental concept. When something, whether it be a jet aircraft or a cake recipe is not working it can almost always come down to three things. They are;

- Too much of something bad
- Not enough of something good
- A combination of the two

For instance, if the car won't run it may be dirt or water in the fuel (bad). Or it may be not enough gas, oil or spark (good).

I know that sounds too simple and obvious, and I am not implying that this is applies to complex ideological problems such as political systems cultural clashes, racism, sexism, etc.

I am talking about mechanical, whether it be biomechanical (plant or animal) or the engine in a car. If you break down a problem to its most fundamental element, 9 out of 10 times when something malfunctions, there will be an excess of a counterproductive component or a lack of an essential component.

It is the same, at the most basic level, with problems of our immune system.

Opinions vary on what is required (beneficial) from one extreme to another. I have heard doctors say "Your body is self-regulating and will do what it does regardless of what you do, and supplements just give you expensive pee." I have also been to the other extreme of the cancer clinic (staffed by MDs) that had me on 58 supplements a day.

I am afraid that there is too much divergence and inconsistency to give any credibility to anything doctors say about nutrition. By the way, most doctors will tell you they got between 2 and 20 hours of nutrition in Med school. But, why would they need more? You don't need any knowledge of nutrition to "diagnose illness and prescribe drugs."

That is why I am writing this. I've been through it, and there is only one reasonable way to address it. Educate yourself and make your own choices. I can tell you, beyond any shadow of a doubt, that there is no prey easier to manipulate for the opportunistic healer, be they mainstream or alternative, than the scared, sick person.

Chapter 29

The ABC's of Cancer - Part 2.

Removing the bad.

We have established that the problems encountered in many things, health included, can often be determined by two factors. Too much damaging or harmful influence, or not enough beneficial influence.

It is critical for me to emphasize, that although this is dealing with cancer, these principles apply to most other chronic diseases as well. But first, the disclaimer:

DISCLAIMER: THIS DOCUMENT DOES NOT PROVIDE MEDICAL ADVICE. The information, including but not limited to text, graphics, images and other material contained in this document, is for informational purposes only. The purpose of this document is to promote broad consumer understanding and knowledge of various health topics. It is not intended to be a substitute for professional medical advice, diagnosis or treatment. Always seek the advice of your physician or other qualified healthcare providers with any questions you may have regarding a medical condition or treatment and before undertaking a new health care regimen, and never disregard professional medical advice or delay in seeking it because of something you have read in this document.

A Garden

If we use a garden as a metaphor, the approach of removing bad and augmenting good becomes quite apparent. In an optimal situation, we want to prepare the environment, which would be the soil. We would start by removing any detrimental items such as weeds, rocks, and try to neutralize any toxic components that we can.

Next, we want to enrich it with the necessary ingredients. Not only the "food" for the plant but also the pH balance, moisture level, etc. Unfortunately, we can't do much about the air the plants breathe, and that goes for us as well. So, there we have it. We have removed as much potential toxicity as possible and provided any additives to create an optimum environment.

Good vibes are also extremely beneficial for humans. I think there are some studies involving that with plants as well, but I haven't researched it.

With regards to our health, the human body itself is the environment. The quality of our health, just as the quality of plants in the garden, is the result of that environment.

Generally speaking, the quality of the environment that is home to the disease (the body itself), is a result of three distinct factors. There are the obvious two, which are nutrition and external environment, and the third, not so obvious, mental and emotional effects.

Now we will get into the process of removing bad and adding good, from a dietary standpoint. We will start with removing the bad.

Sugar

Dr. Otto Warburg was nominated for the Nobel prize three times and won in 1931 for his work in cell respiration. Probably his most notable discovery came in finding that cancer cells have a fundamentally different energy metabolism compared to healthy cells. Without getting too technical, it means that cancer cells utilize glucose more directly and without as much oxygen as do normal cells.

It has not been proven that simply removing all sugar from the diet would cure cancer. However, it has been shown that high quantities of glucose in the blood do allow cancer to grow and flourish as opposed to just "surviving."

At the minimum, we are trying not to give cancer cells an all-you-can-eat buffet. We want to control glucose in a narrow range and avoid spikes that affect insulin response.

Aside from the direct feeding of cancer, sugar compromises body chemistry and the immune system so profoundly that its use contributes to many diseases.

Bottom line: Refined sugars (sugar, corn sweetener, agave, etc.) are straight up poison. They stress the body, create acidity, cause inflammation, and are very addictive as well. They are not even an option for healthy people who want to stay that way.

Processed carbs (grains, etc.) are often just as bad, and even excessive fruit should be restricted in cancer patients. I won't get into the glycemic index, insulin resistance and other related points, but if you have cancer or know someone with cancer, you or they should become thoroughly educated on this subject.

Simple answer? Don't eat any refined sugars or processed carbs. Easy on the fruit, and keep your carbs non-GMO, complex, in their natural state, and organic if possible.

If you honestly do this, you will lose weight through the reduced caloric intake and improved metabolism. For overall improved health and as needed, replace the calories lost from eliminating all the crap with high-quality fats. These can be taken either directly in form such as added to smoothies, coffee (bulletproof coffee) or on salads or other foods. Fats can also be had through foods such as avocado, nuts, etc.

What are high-quality fats? Unprocessed non-GMO preferably organic. Olive oil, coconut, MCT, and butter are some of the most basic, but there are many others.

Fats provide efficient slow-burn energy. They won't create glucose and cause insulin spikes like processed carbs and sugar. If you remove bad carbs and increase quality fat intake, you will radically reduce inflammation in the body regardless of your health.

As for fats, as I mentioned before that it has just been officially released in a study by Tufts University in Massachusetts that butter has been exonerated. The study involving 600,000 people over a 20-year period concluded that butter had no effect, positive or negative, on any type of disease.

The study found mostly small or insignificant associations of each daily serving of butter with total mortality, cardiovascular disease, and diabetes. The "butter eaters" involved averaged three tablespoons a day.

Organic coconut oil, olive oil and other high-quality, natural saturated fats are, no doubt, the same. We, the unsuspecting consumer, have been deceived by the powers that be for decades regarding the truth of fats and cholesterol.

The "sugar feeds cancer" concept is so commonly accepted in Europe and other countries that therapies are built around the glucose uptake of cancer cells. Yet in this country oncologists have no problem recommending milkshakes and candy to chemo patients to help them maintain weight. *There are medical doctors who consider this lack of nutritional understanding, and the resulting health problems it creates, to border on malpractice.*

pH

Cancer likes an acid environment. It does not like an alkaline environment. While I can't endorse or disprove this as a therapy, there are cancer survivors who have used natural treatments and believe that the main reason for their remission was creating and maintaining a healthy alkaline pH. in the body.

The acidity or alkalinity of a substance is measured using pH. The pH scale runs from 0 to 14, with 0 being the most acidic, 14 being the most alkaline, and 7 being neutral. In order to survive, our bodies must maintain the pH very close to 7.4, which is just on the alkaline side of neutral. If your body's pH varies too much from this ideal, it becomes difficult for various enzymes to function properly.

Maintaining this slightly alkaline state is a constant challenge, primarily because of the acid-forming functions that take place within the body, and the overabundance of acid-producing foods and drinks we consume. Excessive acidity has been linked to the formation of heart disease, diabetes, and osteoporosis, as well as cancer.

Maintaining optimal pH in the body is simply a process of eating and drinking alkaline-producing food and beverages, and avoiding heavily acid-producing ones. You can find many charts online, that will give you that information, as well as how to easily test your pH.

Some will argue, "Your body must maintain a specific pH anyway, or you will die. Yes, this is true, but we want to make maintaining the high end of that pH range as easy for the body as possible. We want to allow the body to sustain optimal chemistry with the *least effort possible,* thus saving metabolic energy for healing and other more beneficial activities.

These two factors, high glucose, and acidic pH create the optimum environment and food source for cancer. It goes without saying that we want to deprive it of these. The challenge here is that we can't just take a pill to do this. Since it is all diet regulated, it requires self-discipline and willpower.

This is where a yoga practice may help. Yoga, like most other healthful habits, requires will and effort to maintain. Using your will is like a muscle. The more it is exercised, the stronger it becomes. The stronger it becomes in some areas of life, the easier it is to use it in other areas of life.

Detoxifying

I have mentioned two of the main dietary aspects that contribute to cancer. There are, of course, others. This chapter is not a "how to lifestyle guide" for treating or addressing your situation. This is meant to be an overview, and the results and aims of eliminating the harmful and adding the beneficial to your body are subjects of entire books.

Eliminating harmful things is not just a case of stopping them in the moment. There are the accumulated harmful elements stored in the fat and tissue of your body. This is where detoxing comes in.

As with diet, there are books written on methods of removing existing toxins from the body. I'm not going to get into the discussion of the validity of fasting, far-infrared saunas, intestinal cleanses, colonics or lymphatic drainage and whatnot. But I will attest from my own detoxing, that I have experienced first-hand the benefits of eliminating toxins from my body.

Residual toxins in the body are not limited to foods eaten in the past. Insecticides, hormones, antibiotics, questionable food additives and all the other things our government allows into the food system are certainly there.

There are many things we can acquire through the water, air, drugs (both pharmaceutical and recreational), dental work, surgeries and other exposures. The detoxification process will address all these. As I said, there is plenty of media addressing detox so pick your poison (pun intended).

In addition to removing these types of toxins, there is also the matter of parasites, metals, chronic low-grade candida, viruses and things of that nature. Those should be considered as well.

This may be appearing overwhelming, but it is not. Like so many things in life, you just take one thing at a time and work through the list.

The process of removing addictive and harmful, yet taste-gratifying food is not easy. Going through detox protocols is not something fun to do. Unfortunately, it is necessary to regain healthy biochemistry and immune system.

Physical methods to aid detox

These types of detox methods include things like massage, lymph drainage, acupuncture, far infrared sauna, specific yoga postures, intestinal cleanses, parasite elimination, colonics and any other method used to help detox through a physical application.

These are great because they are more passive, and don't require as much energy and effort from the patient. They are, however, not "stand-alone" remedies. Diet is essential.

Chapter 30

The ABCs of Cancer - Part 3

Adding the good.

We have discussed removing the bad, now on to adding the beneficial. This will be supplementation, treatments, and exercise;

When talking about supplements, there are three primary groups to consider;

- Components that occur in quality food and water.

- Components that exist in and are produced by our body but may be compromised.

- Items that exist in nature that have healing or medicinal properties.

Most people consider vitamins to be the only necessary supplement. This, however, is not the case.

You can have all the nutrients possible in food, but they are useless if your body cannot assimilate them. This brings us to the subject of gut health. Without the gut and digestive system working well, the nutrients in food and supplements are useless.

The subject of gut health is now very much in vogue. I find it interesting that the obviousness importance of the system that assimilates and absorbs the nutrients we consume was not addressed for so long by progressive health practitioners, much less traditional medical doctors.

At any rate, now it is recognized that the gut and the brain are in constant communication regulating all kinds of necessary bodily functions.

Chew your food

Just like your mama might have told you, "Chew your food." This is where gut health begins. Digestion begins in your mouth. Chewing signals digestive enzyme release, breaks down food structure, exposes the food to saliva enzymes, makes digestion more efficient, is good for your teeth, and may help you to eat less if weight is a problem. You can read all about the value of "proper mastication" on the Internet.

Intestinal flora

To most people, the most commonly known part of a healthy gut is beneficial bacteria, also known as intestinal flora. It is also one of the most compromised systems in our bodies, thanks to antibiotics. The problem is not limited to antibiotics that we have taken, but also second-hand antibiotics from consuming factory farmed meat and dairy, as well as pesticide exposure.

The first step is to remove these from your diet. If you want meat and dairy, and healthy vegetables, buy organic.

The next step is to take high-quality gut health supplements such as probiotics and eat beneficial foods. These foods would include, fermented foods such as sauerkraut or not excessively sweet kombucha. A container of commercially produced sugary yogurt is not going to do anything.

The emphasis here should be on quality. In this world, you get what you pay for. That is just how it is. Here are some words to remember. *"You can either spend your money at the grocery store or spend it at the doctor's office."*

If you have been on a course of antibiotics, you need to focus on supplements and the right foods to rebuild intestinal flora.

Digestive aids and enzymes

These would include digestive enzymes and hydrochloric acid. Both occur naturally but may be compromised for a number of reasons. I tend to use them depending on what I am eating. If I have a smoothie, I may take nothing. If I'm having a big or rich meal, I dose up.

The use of other enzymes (such as pancreatic or proteolytic) in treating diseases is a science in itself.

As with any of these supplements, it is best to have expert nutritional guidance and testing to determine what and how much of what you should be taking.

Vitamins and minerals

People often think of vitamins when they think of "supplements," but minerals are just as important. The fact that, in a perfect world, we would be getting minerals from many plant food sources and water makes this a problem.

These days most health-conscious people drink bottled water. It has been filtered to remove harmful chemicals, but the filtering process also removes beneficial minerals. Between that and non-organic plant foods, we don't get nearly enough minerals. This is compounded if you are in a situation where you sweat frequently.

When it comes to vitamins and minerals, quantity over quality is not the answer. It is far better to have smaller doses of *high-quality,* easily absorbed and utilized vitamin and mineral supplements than vast amounts of cheap synthetic products. Also, lower doses of quality supplements are less taxing on the liver.

That is all I am going to say about vitamins, minerals, and digestive aids. If you want to do this right, you will need a highly-qualified and forward-thinking nutritionist who has reliable ways to test for your deficiencies.

Herbs and medicinal plants.

These types of supplements include items that are not required for healthy nutrition but have specific healing properties. Things such as herbs, plants, mushrooms, essential oils, and extracts make up this group. There are literally hundreds, if not thousands of naturally occurring medicinal items and compounds.

The application of these types of healing substances is a very specialized field. You want a naturopath with much experience. Here again, a reliable way to test for your individual needs is essential.

Exercise

Exercise is something we need that adds good, benefiting the body, as well as removing bad by helping to detoxify the body. One of the critical ingredients to exercise is now seen as "movement."

Common functional movement such as walking, pushing, pulling and lifting is now considered to be highly beneficial. The thought is that after countless generations of human existence, our bodies have adapted and will respond well to these fundamental human movements.

The level of intensity of these movements is easy to adjust to the level of a person's health. For people in bad shape, it is not necessary to lift anything heavy. Walking could be done with a walker or cane. The goal is to move. It is amazing the rate at which the human body can improve with just a little focused effort.

This is not a five-minute attempt, and then off to the couch for some TV. At a minimum, most people should start with 20 minutes of something manageable, and work up to at least 30-40 minutes five or six times a week.

Yoga

First off, I need to preface this with something. What commonly passes for "yoga" these days is, overall, not very good. As I discuss the following subject, all of this assumes a teacher who has much experience and knowledge. This is not the case with many "newly minted" yoga teachers out there.

The beauty of yoga is that, on the physical level, it is a physical activity that can be adjusted and tailored to any level of fitness or physical condition.

There are some benefits of yoga that set it apart from other forms of exercise. One benefit is the specific effect of certain postures on different organs, the nervous system, connective tissue, blood flow, and other body functions.

For instance, if you were dealing with such diverse issues as digestive problems, liver problems, scoliosis, sciatica, or many other conditions, there are postures that can target and help. One example would be forward bends and twists that can stimulate and bring blood flow to different organs.

There is also the focus on the breath. Of all the things required for human life, none is more essential than breath. Surprisingly, even by medical standards, many people don't breathe with great efficiency. Well-taught yoga emphasizes correct and appropriate breathing.

Lastly, as I have mentioned, the mental and spiritual aspects of true yoga are highly beneficial. I will cover more on that a little later.

Part Four
The Bottom Line

Chapter 31

Preparation is Key

> *"Luck is what happens when preparation meets opportunity." – Seneca*

I hope that you have read and gained some valuable knowledge regarding Cancer. However, in spite of the relevant information, the point and illustration of that section of this book is in the depth of research that should be done.

As I have said before, the opponents (some may prefer to consider them teachers) that arise in this world are many and varied. They may come in the form of physical illnesses, which are many. They may be mental or emotional conditions such as depression, anxiety, PTSD, bipolar or addiction. They may be problems or situations such as divorce, legal issues, or unhealthy relationships.

It all comes back to Sun Tsu. You must know your enemy and everything about it, in great depth.

It is very tempting and easy to turn over all control to someone we consider an "expert," and hope for the best. I am not saying don't seek expert help. Always use the best resources and people you can find to help you, and that may take a lot of research as well.

The point is to avoid being the uninformed helpless person. You need to understand what is happening, what is being done, why it is being done and what are all the possible options.

You want to be that client, patient or customer who is always asking, "Why?" and "What are all the options and their potential risks and rewards, what else could I be doing?" Then research and understand those options.

I hope I have made it clear that this is not just a choice between traditional methods and alternative methods in approaching a condition or situation. There is much conflicting information regarding anything you encounter, and it is entirely up to you to learn all you can, and then make your best choices.

Nobody has your best interests at heart the way you do. Don't give up your power.

Chapter 32

Where Do We Go from Here?

> *"Do what you can, with what you have, where you are". Theodore Roosevelt*

We have come to the moment of truth.

We have some perspective on the arena of life.

We understand the different facets of yoga.

We have a clear understanding of the opponent.

We will put together strategies to address the problem from the three primary components of the human experience.

- Physical
- Mental
- Spiritual

These are relevant to any significant problem, although each individual problem will be weighted differently.

For instance, while working on a physical condition, more emphasis may be directed at the physical problem and supported by the others. A problem such as depression or addiction may have more focus on the mental, or possibly spiritual, and be supported by the others.

However, most often problems are best handled by addressing all three components. The physically embodied human is a composite of all three forces, whether aware of them or not.

Any plan to address any problem or battle will do far better with a strategy. A well-formed plan, approach, and prioritization of energy is necessary for success. Strategies are not written in stone. They are fluid and malleable depending on changing circumstances, but that does not mean they are loose or undisciplined.

Let's have a look at some options and ideas for these strategies.

The Physical Components

When dealing with a serious physical situation, it can become very overwhelming and confusing. Part of the problem is that there may be contradictory approaches and opinions by not only alternative practitioners but traditional medicine as well.

Assuming you have done your research, it is time to "pick your poison" and commit to your choices. The temptation is to throw everything you can at the problem, but the better choice is to narrow it down and prioritize options. Make choices that you feel give the most return on investment of your time, energy and money.

This is not necessarily a question of money, although that could be a concern. It is a question of being able to manage the time and energy required for what you are doing. It is very tempting to jump in with physical therapy/exercise, diet, nutritional supplements and detox protocols along with mental/emotional work. But trying to do too many things soon leads to burnout.

Taking supplements throughout the day, managing diet, physical work, meditation or therapy, and going for treatments all require time, energy, and discipline. Biting off too much, as with so many other things in life, often ends in becoming overwhelmed and giving up.

You must be specific in the time you schedule for what you are doing, and stay focused on those things.

Diet

Unfortunately, unless you can afford a personal chef, eating a wholesome and healing diet involves a lot more than just changing your order at the McDonald's drive-through.

The biggest energy expended will be on shopping and preparation of food. It is very challenging to get genuinely high-quality food at most restaurants. That means shopping for quality ingredients, and having the time to prepare them is essential.

What usually happens is you will find healthy dishes that are relatively simple to prepare, and then use variations on those recipes.

Most healing diets are heavy in plant-based foods. That means shopping more often for freshness, and more time cutting, cleaning and cooking. That is just how it is, and becoming efficient in this is a learned skill. Keep things simple and healthy as you build your skills. It can be a fun and rewarding adventure learning about food and creating dishes that will produce better health, vitality, energy and an improved emotional state.

Diet and Emotions

Just because your problem may be emotional does not mean you get a free ride on diet.

It has been shown in many case studies that there is a direct link between nutrition and mental state. When your body is in balance, you can't help but feel better.

A proper diet and a devoted exercise program have been enough to change the lives of many people suffering from depression, anxiety, addiction and other emotional issues.

Exercise

One of the most challenging things to allow time for, and stick to, is exercise.

Within the realm of exercise are three main components;

- Strength
- Flexibility
- Cardiovascular health.

It requires a great deal of time and energy to address all three of these at a high level. Most people excel at one or two and let the others slide somewhat, and that is okay.

The key to an effective approach to exercise requires one primary ingredient. You must enjoy and look forward to the activity. Without that, you are doomed to failure. Making the time to maintain a regular exercise program is hard enough, even when you look forward to it.

The second consideration is that it must not be at a level of difficulty that overwhelms or discourages you. The temptation in our society is buying into the "more is more" mentality. More is not more if it ends with you being overwhelmed, discouraged, and giving up.

In a physical or mental recovery situation, we are not looking for peak athletic performance. We are looking for physical support and improved health. If this leads to pursuing a high level of some physical activity, that's fine. But the goal, in the beginning should be to find something you want to do, show up for, and which will give you the result you need on that day, at that moment.

I often tell my yoga students they did as much "yoga" by showing up to class as they will do on the mat. The mental effort and willpower that it takes to make the time, get in the car, drive to class and deal with whatever cleanup is required afterward is a discipline.

Discipline in one aspect of life can develop and support discipline in other parts of your life, and as much as it may sound like an oxymoron, *discipline leads to freedom.*

Of course, for exercise, I always recommend yoga. In my life, I have explored many, many types of physical activity, and some for long periods of time. But yoga is the one that I have always maintained and has been with me through it all.

Supplements

As odd as it may sound, managing supplements can be challenging. When you begin on a path of supplementation, it is very easy to get to the point of taking a lot of pills a day.

The problem is that many must be taken throughout the day. Some need to be taken on an empty stomach, and some with food; Some when you wake up, and some at bedtime.

In addition, supplements come in bottles of different quantities and are taken in varying amounts, so staying ahead of running out of different ones at different rates takes thought and effort.

My point is that managing 20 to 50 pills a day takes planning and energy.

Most people find breaking supplements down into containers for daily use works best. There are different ways to do this, but I find the commercially available containers with compartments easiest for me.

Sitting down with all your bottles and dividing things up for the week, or whatever time span you choose takes some time. Here again, the key is not to jump into an overwhelming program that will discourage you. Keep things at a manageable level. Choose and use the most important supplements for your needs, and add or remove them as necessary.

Some research and control on your part may very well be necessary. The health practitioner you see will often be quite willing to sell you as many products as possible. Aside from the additional revenue, there usually is a value to each different supplement.

However, some supplements are far more necessary to your specific needs than others, and it is up to you to decide how much you can deal with. If you start getting into the 40+ pills per day, taken at seven different times throughout the day, it is not easy.

Physical Treatments

Here is where you can get into spending a lot of time and money. Obviously, if insurance is covering it, the costs will be far less. However, the time commitment is the same.

Even with conventional treatment, chemo and radiation can be 40, 60 or 90 days of daily or weekly treatments, but there also may be recovery time involved during and after.

As either a compliment to traditional medical treatment or as stand-alone protocols, alternative therapies and treatments require much time and expense. There are so many to research, and a competent health practitioner or progressive doctor is needed to help direct you.

Alternative treatments include, but are not limited to:

- Various IV drips
- Hyperthermia
- Hyperbaric oxygen
- Far infrared sauna
- Massage and reflexology
- Lymph drainage massage
- Acupuncture
- Different therapies for dealing with stress, anxiety, etc.

These all require time and travel and need to be managed. Again, narrow it down to the essentials and do what you can handle.

As I have mentioned before, stress is at the root of so many diseases. It is critical that your healing program does not cause excessive stress or anxiety. Excessive stress will outweigh the benefits, and you will be wasting your time and money.

Mental

The power of the human mind is extraordinary. It is unfortunate that the pervasive culture of this planet is so focused on selling us on limitation rather than power. Of course, it makes sense that those who possess knowledge and power prefer others not to have it. This gives them temporary ego gratification for the briefest of moments, in a reality of illusion, that ultimately means no more than a dream.

Most people live in prisons of self-limitation. It isn't any fault of theirs. Most of us are products of our environment and cannot see beyond the horizon of our own experience.

Words have so much power, and I am an avid believer in the value of verbal affirmation. I have seen it work first-hand, and yet I am continually amazed at the degree to which people unconsciously use their words to reinforce their limitations. Why would one do that when it is just as easy to speak to your power?

Many people believe and use the power of affirmation. They use it as an applied method of self-improvement, and to create an improved reality for themselves. They may have a vision board and a list of daily affirmations. Yet in their everyday conversation, dialogue, and attitude they project and affirm limitation.

"I'm ok. I'm hanging in there. It is what it is. I have (fill in the blank) ailment. I'm exhausted. I'm tired. I'm stressed." Please notice that this type of conversation and dialogue is a constant negative affirmation.

When it comes to disease, I never say, "I *have...*" I say, "*I was diagnosed with...*" There is a distinct difference. One implies currently possessing. The other implies past tense. Whether the problem is currently active or not is irrelevant to the conversation. I'm not going to give it the power of verbal affirmation.

Stress: Attack the Most Dangerous Enemy First

I hope by now it is clear that I, as well as many others, consider stress to be the greatest cause of most physical and emotional problems, or as they could be called, "symptoms." Stress is at the root of so many problems and can manifest many different symptoms.

It should be apparent that of all the things we are dealing with on an emotional level, managing stress should be the first and primary objective. Here is a partial list of some of the more common methods people use to deal with stress:

- Exercise.
- Meditation

- Talk therapy
- Tapping (EFT)
- EVOX
- Biofeedback.

There are, of course, others. The primary consideration is to find what works for you and hit dealing with stress first, fast and hard. *Without taking the head off the snake, nothing else will ultimately matter.* If you are dealing with a physical situation, managing stress must be addressed while engaging in chosen therapies.

If your situation is in the realm of addiction, depression, anxiety, etc., then in addition to stress management, specific therapies to address your needs should be included. This could involve separate treatments for the particular problem or twelve-step programs and things like that.

Don't forget that diet, and exercise should be part of healing emotional issues as well. In addition, many find happiness in things like creative pursuits, serving others, and fellowship. Stay engaged and productive. It is a cliché but also true: what you give is what you get.

All of what I have talked about so far involves proactive, added activities as part of dealing with stress and as an aid to healing. Now we must address what needs to be removed. Separating yourself from toxic situations can be the most painful and challenging part of managing stress.

This is because we are often very attached to sources of high stress in our lives. Separating ourselves from people, places, jobs, situations, and even family is sometimes the only choice. It can be brutal to say to someone, "We've been through so much, and it's not anyone's fault, but this (relationship, job, arrangement, etc.) is literally killing me."

Often this will result in much drama, back-peddling, professing love, changing of ways, not understanding, and all of that. But if you've been in it enough to know the routine, you have no choice. Your life may depend on it.

Almost everyone I've talked to who is successfully dealing with being a survivor of a disease or serious problems says the same thing, "I don't do people or situations that cause me stress. I just can't go there."

Does this mean your life will be stress-free? Of course not, but the hope is that you will deal with the daily, uncontrollable sources of stress. but you won't knowingly put yourself in harm's way.

The Specific Situation

The next aspect of mental/emotional treatment targets the specifics of the enemy.

As I mentioned before, there are programs and support groups for every problem. There is usually not a downside to trying legitimate programs to see if one, or more, may serve you. Fellowship, accountability, and education can be very helpful to many people.

I would also consider affirmation and visualization, specific to your situation, to be very valuable. I have seen and experienced the positive results of affirmation and visualization too many times to doubt their effectiveness. There are many good books describing methods of visualization and affirmation. But, here again, the book on the shelf or in your Kindle is useless if you don't do the work.

Spiritual

This will be short.

The idea of spirituality and religion are so closely associated that for most people there is often a lot of emotional baggage, content, opinion, resentment, and other negative things associated with them. Mama always told me don't discuss religion and politics.

That said, I have experienced many conversations and written and recorded testimonials by people who have survived a deadly disease or overcome a serious emotional disorder or problem.

A vast percentage of these people profess a deep faith in a higher power. What that is for anyone is not my place to define. It is just an observation, based on my research, and you are free to take that information as you wish.

Now, for the personal. I began my journey on the spiritual path a long time ago. It has ebbed and flowed in its intensity and application. However, even when I have been lax or inattentive to it, the relationship with Spirit is always close to my heart.

I have experienced that world of Spirit, and felt its relief and comfort many times. I, personally, could not imagine facing the horrific scenarios this creation manifests without that connection.

Finding Happiness

Any of the techniques talked about up to now would also be well used directed toward the task of finding happiness.

In the same way that stress triggers a negative hormonal response in the body, happiness triggers health and healing. When we experience joy and pleasure, our emotions are signaling that we are in a safe, non-threatening environment. This is obviously the exact opposite of fight or flight and stress mode.

It is during these times that the body's hormone balance goes into rest, repair and growth mode. This is where we want to be as often as possible. Laughter, fun with people, love, art and all the things that bring lightness and joy should be consciously sought.

But, of course, there is a catch.

We, especially in the west, live in a consumer-driven society. We are programmed and reprogrammed continuously to think happiness will come to us from sources outside ourselves. This is usually sought in the form of material objects and other people.

This is the biggest deception we are living with. It is true that objects and people bring temporary satisfaction and happiness, but they also bring sadness and sorrow. It is, again, the nature of attachment and duality in this world.

It is a regularly cited cliché, but you have got to find happiness inside yourself. It has been extolled, over and over, in everything from spiritual scripture to poetry, movies, and rock 'n' roll.

Naturally, possessions and people can bring happiness that comes and goes, and should be enjoyed when present. But beneath it all, you should do whatever work you need to do to bring yourself out of negativity and into positivity.

I know it may seem like an impossible task to many people, but you can argue for your limitations or for your power. Which argument do you want to win?

I have walked a path of extremes at times in my life. I have had a lot and lost a lot. I know people who have made millions and lost it all. I have talked to them and others about the experience of having so much and if it made the core person, who they are and how they feel any happier. They all said, "No."

It has been shown in studies that once the fear of financial survival and comfort is alleviated, more money and possessions do not improve people's state of mind.

I don't have a prescription for you here, but I will say this. You should make finding happiness and satisfaction from within a very, very high priority in your life.

Chapter 33

The Human Condition

> *"The legacy of heroes is the memory of a great name and the inheritance of a great example. - Benjamin Disraeli*

Wikipedia defines "The Human Condition" as "The characteristics, key events, and situations which compose the essentials of human existence, such as birth, growth, emotionality, aspiration, conflict, and mortality. This is a very broad topic which has been and continues to be pondered and analyzed from many perspectives, including those of religion, philosophy, history, art, literature, anthropology, psychology, and biology."

I find it interesting that, in the past, different physical and mental illnesses and maladies were also referred to as "conditions." These were often situations that didn't have clear-cut remedies or cures. Things that people lived with, and hopefully overcame, on a day-to-day basis.

Evidently, being human is comparable to living with certain shortcomings and issues that need to be overcome and dealt with on an ongoing and never-ending basis. And really, that is not far off the mark.

If you happen to believe in reincarnation, never-ending takes on a whole new meaning.

Despite how some people's lives may appear, no one is getting a free ride. We all wake up to the same arena or battleground. We live with the demands of a physical body, the voice in our head, and the complexities of relationships with others and the environment that surrounds us.

But, perhaps, the most challenging part of dealing with these things is the tendency of the "human condition" to take us into less beneficial choices. Things like not eating the foods we should, or passing on that yoga class or a trip to the gym.

We can all find our way during times of need or inspiration. It's keeping it going in the long term, mundane, everyday existence that is the challenge.

I have taught yoga to thousands of people over the years. I have seen them come for years and make tremendous gains, physically and mentally. I have had them tell me, "You and yoga changed my life."

And then one day they are gone. Or their coming to class gets less and less frequent. Sometimes they drop out and then make a few sporadic returns, and then disappear. I have done exactly this myself, at times, when it comes to the gym.

I sometimes run into them months or years later. I can see the light in them diminished from the time of their disciplined practice. We chat, and it is often the same story, "This, and that happened, and this changed, and, yeah I really need to get back into it."

This is someone who at one time said, "Yoga changed my life." Beneath it all, even they seem unsure of what happened.

That is part of the "human condition," that strange quality of life that so subtly clouds our awareness and takes us to different and usually more superficial interests. It is almost like hypnosis. It is what the yogis refer to as "Maya."

From the yoga perspective, Maya is the human condition. It continually draws us into the physical and sense-oriented distractions of life, and that is okay. That is what we are here for- to engage in this creation. The problems come when we forget that it is a game and we are just spirit players in the game and not the roles we play.

And that is the real value of what yoga is for me. It could be a different spiritual practice as well, for someone else. But, it is the process that allows one to realize oneself as the player of the game, and not to be "played" by the game.

Notice that I said, "realize." This is a quality that cannot be learned intellectually or memorized. It must be experienced first-hand to be understood. That experience comes from "doing the work."

It may be your spiritual practice or a specific problem of physical or mental health. It could be an intense fight for your life or just daily maintenance. Whatever the challenge, it is the continuous "doing the work" that matters.

So, what is the answer to maintaining the effort? To prevent ourselves from becoming cloudy, forgetful, and distracted by less beneficial activities? It is an approach we can exercise and use that is simple in concept, yet harder in practice:

- Constant vigilance
- Constant resolve

Vigilance is the essence of the practice that keeps us on track.

In yoga, introspection and self-assessment are the keys to vigilance. It is no coincidence that the very first verse of the Bhagavad Gita represents the act of self-evaluation. It is the conscious questioning of one's behavior, discipline and attitude regarding whatever situation we are in.

Resolve is the discipline to act on improving the things that need work and maintaining the ones that are working. Resolve is the dedication and willpower to "do the work."

These are not skills that are learned and then filed away. These are like muscles that need to be used every day, or they will atrophy and become useless.

If you can remember to apply these qualities to your life, regardless of your needs at the moment, you will have a far greater chance at success.

I don't know if what Benjamin Disraeli says, at the beginning of this chapter means much to most people. An immortal legacy is not everyone's goal. I do however think that to live life with the idea of a positive, uplifting, legacy is a noble path indeed.

Whatever the pursuit may be...health, money, relationships, personal growth, it doesn't matter. If you can apply daily vigilance and resolve to your goals, you can succeed.

This is what I will leave you with, vigilance and resolve. Two practices that have served me, and many others very well. Apply them for a while and see what happens.

> *"And in the end, the love you take is equal to the love you make." - The Beatles*

The last topic I will remind you of is the idea of giving. For whatever reasons, it seems to be the case that what you put out into life influences what you receive.

It is no harder to put out love, respect, or compassion to others than to put out contempt, ego superiority, or indifference. It is, ultimately, a choice that you are continually making and exercising.

As easy as it is to blame others for your behavior and situation, in the end, it is really up to you and the choices you make. By understanding, acknowledging and dealing with your part in your circumstance, you have left the "victim mindset" behind. You are now poised to do battle, as a warrior, against the demons of "the human condition." Hopefully, in that role, you can also bring light and inspiration to others.

There you have it. I hope that, out of all these pages, you have found something to help you. Something that educated or motivated you. Moved or inspired you. Maybe reminded you of something of value that you had forgotten.

Whether your task is physical, mental, emotional, material, or spiritual I sincerely wish you all the success and happiness this world can give.

About the Author

credit to nataliafabia.com

David Danon was born in Pasadena, California in the middle of the 20th century. As it was for many during that time, he was unknowingly recruited as a participant in the social upheaval of the 1960's. The outcome of this was a deep questioning of authority and the status quo.

He traveled extensively, sailed around the world, and has pursued many sports and physical activities. He is a licensed pilot, musician, has built motorcycles, has done woodworking, leatherwork, and painting, among other creative pursuits. He co-founded a clothing company, and worked in the Film and Television industry for 20 years.

He was exposed to yoga at a young age by his mother. He began practicing yoga asana and meditation as an adult over 40 years ago, long before it was the broadly accepted culture that exists today. He began teaching yoga in 1997. This is, and has been the foundation of his approach and view of the world for most of his adult life.

After a cancer diagnosis in 2012 he embarked on a journey of research and experimentation into the world of traditional and alternative treatments of cancer and other chronic disease. In his own words, "I know way more about cancer and the system that treats it than I ever wanted to know."

For more go to lifeyogaandcancer.com

77535257R00146

Made in the USA
San Bernardino, CA
24 May 2018